RECOGNITION

THE
QUALITY
WAY

Toni La Motta

QR QUALITY RESOURCES ®
A Division of The Kraus Organization Limited
902 Broadway, New York, New York 10010

Most Quality Resources books are available at quantity discounts when purchased in bulk. For more information contact:

Special Sales Department
Quality Resources
A Division of The Kraus Organization Limited
902 Broadway
New York, New York 10010
800-247-8519

Printed in the United States of America

99 98 97 96 95   10 9 8 7 6 5 4 3 2 1

Quality Resources
A Division of The Kraus Organization Limited
902 Broadway
New York, New York 10010
800-247-8519

∞

The paper used in this publication meets the minimum requirements of American National Standard for Information Sciences—Permanence of Paper for Printed Library Materials, ANSI Z39.48-1984.

ISBN 0-527-76223-7

Library of Congress Cataloging-in-Publication Data

LaMotta, Toni.
    Recognition / Toni LaMotta.
        p.   cm.
    ISBN 0-527-76223-7
    1. Employee motivation.   2. Recognition (Psychology).   3. Employee morale.   4. Total quality management.   I. Title.
HF5549.5.M63L36 1995
658.3'14—dc20   95-1339
                                                                          CIP

To my teachers and students—
who I recognize are one and the same.

CONTENTS

ACKNOWLEDGMENTS

I stand on the shoulders of many giants who have gone before me in the fields of motivation, change, understanding differences, learning theory, and spiritual philosophy. While I have not agreed with all I've read and heard throughout the years, I am grateful for the critical reflection it afforded me so that I could come to a clearer statement of my own Truth. I acknowledge that there is but One Mind, and I am grateful to Spirit for my individual expression.

Though all of my students over the past few years have had influence on my thinking and writing, I want to particularly thank the students from the University of Phoenix, San Diego and ONLINE who contributed to the research and who may hear their own words echoed in this book. They are: Jackie Anderson, Mary Ellen Bed, Kelly Bride, Dean, Crystal Chilean Kroeger, Jennifer Cassidy, Brad Fradella, Fred Garcia, Angela Goossen, Elizabeth Jones, Daniel Kilburn, Yvonne Lopez, Pat Needham, Marcel Raterman, Beth Shannon, Christina Stahler, Carlos Velasquez, Guy Venuti, Jason Wheeler and Anne Williamson.

A special thank you goes to Hollis Barnhart, the acquisitions editor at Quality Resources, who believed in my idea, supported my rewrites, and extended deadlines with the utmost patience.

So many clients have encouraged me by putting my ideas into practice and so many friends have supported me in my personal process. Thank you for being there: Marie Picciuto, Judy Lukin, Pam Kilbourne, Sheila Felber, Cheryl Defendorf, and Jan Bartlett. Thanks to Riley and Riches, my feline companions, who sat by my side (or on the keyboard!) through the whole process. And, a special thanks to Rev. Kathy Hearn for helping me to "just do it" and experience the joy of completion!

INTRODUCTION

"The deepest principle in human nature is the craving to be appreciated."

—William James

"The deepest urge in human nature is the desire to be important."

—Prof. John Dewey

"Everyone wants to be great."

—Sigmund Freud

"By appreciating, we make excellence in others our own property."

—Voltaire

"There are two things that people want more than sex and money—that's praise and recognition."

—Mary Kay Ash

"We are motivated by a keen desire for praise and the better a person is, the more he/she is inspired by glory."

—*Cicero*

"The deafest person can hear praise, and is slow to think any an excess."

—*Walter Savage Landor*

"It is a great sign of mediocrity to praise always moderately."

—*Vauvenargues*

There's no doubt in my mind (and in my experience) that people don't get all the recognition that they want, need, and deserve. When they do feel recognized, it usually comes from some committee or outside activity that they joined or some community service organization in which they took a leadership role. It very seldom comes to them on the job and in fact is one of the major causes of job dissatisfaction today.

Is there a parallel between this lack of recognition and the lack of quality and excellence that we have seen? In recent times, there has been a loud call from authors, speakers, and corporate gurus to bring back quality into the workplace. We've heard talk of quality circles and quality of life, but from what I've read and seen, we still seem to be talking about improving products and processes—and missing the *people* that perform the processes and produce these products. Excellence and quality are still something we *strive for* rather than a common experience in the workplace. It's time we take a serious look at least one major underlying issue to understand why. Until we learn how to truly value people, in all their uniqueness—and let them know it in ways they can accept and understand—we'll forever be fixing symptoms without getting to the root of the problem.

Most people stay in jobs not for the money received, but because they believe that *what* they say and *who* they are makes a difference. Many companies give out gold watches or plaques or have picnics and luncheons to celebrate anniversaries and goal successes. However, employees increasingly complain (and change jobs) because they don't perceive that they've been recognized. Although they are tangible rewards, pay raises and bonuses only motivate for a brief time; studies show that productivity increases can be directly attributed to how much employees feel that they are seen, heard, and understood. Recognition is one of our most basic needs and as such, must be addressed in the place we spend most of our lives—at work.

Psychologist Abraham Maslow spoke of human beings having a hierarchy of needs with the most basic being survival. These needs include things like food, clothing, and shelter. Other psychologists talk of the need for work, or belonging, or fun as the things that are most fundamental to our self-esteem. At the heart of what most of us are seeking in life is an acknowledgment of our *being*. We want to be known. We want to be seen and heard. When we realize that we truly exist for someone else, on a new level we begin to exist for ourselves. It is what can truly empower us. We may each find unique ways of expressing it, but our common core need is to be recognized.

Don't you want to contribute and be acknowledged for your contribution? Pride in workmanship seems to be an inborn drive. Companies often rob employees of this sense of accomplishment by the very systems they create to try to inculcate it. Reward and merit systems, annual ratings, and review are among the means companies have used in the past. We need new paradigms, new models of behaviors, attitudes, and structures so that recognition will be a prevailing attitude rather than a once in a while—oh, by the way—occurrence.

Often, people who leave companies after only a short period of employment are the highest producers. They leave behind employees who are mediocre workers. They leave not for the proverbial "offer they couldn't refuse", but in the hopes that their new place of employment or their entrepreneurial experience will give them what they've been looking for—a voice, a chance to be heard, an awareness of what really makes them special and unique, and what contributions only they can offer. Recently, I was talking with someone who said she left for that proverbial better offer. Upon probing more deeply, however, she began to tell me that she left because her new employer told her she had a great personality—one that they truly needed on the job she was being offered. No one had said that to her in her previous job at a major hotel chain where they otherwise pride themselves for employee recognition programs. People may not always voice it directly, but most often they leave seeking the recognition they some-how failed to receive. This often happens despite the pay raises and promotions or occasional kudos and "attaboys" that were handed to them sporadically.

According to the American Productivity and Quality Center, 91% of all employees value recognition above other remuneration. Only about half say they feel that they are recognized at all. Recognition is essential to employees and by extension, to organizations. Unfortunately, recognition is often seen as something that is *nice* to do rather than as something that we *need* to do. When companies learn to un-derstand what motivates and how to recognize employees, greater job satisfaction will result. This concept is at the core of total quality management (TQM). Exceptional leaders have discovered that TQM has far broader implication than simply creating quality products. Although these are important if America is to *survive* in a global marketplace, to *thrive* we need nothing short of a transformation of the very philosophy by which we have been managing. As Deming exhorted, we must move from a position of managing *results* and processing data to finding the delicate interaction of *people*, technology, products, and the environment. There is no short cut to quality. To make it truly happen, organizational cultures must change at their core. Quality must become a habit in everything that is done and said. To this end, recognition must not simply be a sometime thing (e.g., a monthly or yearly practice), but an all-pervading attitude that people can count on—both the people who make up the inner working (the employees) and the vendors and customers, without whom there would be no business.

My purpose in writing this book is to motivate companies to take a closer look at *people* as their most important resource, and to acknowledge that people are the key to any success in creating a truly quality-oriented climate. I will highlight the need for recognition to become a fundamental part of the corporate culture, personality, and philosophy of the organization rather than being given lip service by offering a raise, bonus, or occasional tangible reward. I offer suggestions for creating an atmosphere where Monday morning heart attacks are nonexistent and no one celebrates Fridays more than any other day.

If your business is already focusing on TQM, this book will provide a practical guide to creating a complete recognition system (not just a program) in your corporations or departments. You will have the opportunity to peer into other organizations and find out what works and what doesn't. And finally, it is my intention to inspire you to become more conscious of even small daily actions that can be effective instruments for change and improved quality of life at work and home for yourselves and others.

WHAT IS RECOGNITION?

Our country's work ethic, and even the move toward TQM, is grounded in a behavioristic philosophy. Companies often focus on changing behavior by punishment and reward. There are consequences for a job not being done, or not being done well. There are rewards when it is perceived that a person or team of people were instrumental in reaching a particular goal. Unfortunately, most people perceive that rewards equal recognition. Although an attitude that looks to reward employees, whether in the "one-minute" style or by ribbons and plaques, far exceeds a punishing mentality, rewards alone don't ensure that a person truly feels recognized.

What then, is quality recognition? It is a paradigm shift in the way that we see the recognition we give employees. For a person to feel true recognition, four essential stages of a total process must be fulfilled:

Stage 1: Awareness

Awareness is becoming conscious of the fact that another person exists—and seeing life from his or her point of view, even when there are deadlines and quotas to be met. It is an attitude of living in the now and taking the time to be present to one another on a daily basis, not just when something outstanding has been accomplished. It's putting people before things and projects—in our lives, and on our jobs. (No tombstone ever said, "I wish I worked harder or contributed more to the bottom line!") The awareness stage allows us to ask ourselves and live as if we believe that the measure of the worth of the quality of our lives is more important than the quality of our products and the quantity of our profits. For many people, the American Dream has become the American nightmare. We are finally waking up and hearing all of the people who keep saying, "Doesn't anyone know I'm here? I'm not just a body or a statistic or an EEO quota. I'm more than brawn. I'm a person with a brain. I take pride in my work. I have a contribution to make to this organization that is unique and special. Please hear me."

Stage 2: Appreciation

Appreciation is saying thank you for a job well done. This includes most of the tangible rewards and incentives presented today by companies. I "recognize" you for a job well done. I may even cite you in a company newsletter or send you flowers. What I've done is temporarily put the focus on you for what you've done for me! A company throws an appreciation banquet for the top sales executives for the past year. "Thank you . . . because of you . . . our company has grown. You did something for **us** and we appreciate it." Subtly, I (or the company) am the focal point, the center of attention, not really you. And so, you may feel good for a while, but something seems missing and it doesn't exactly change your life.

Most of the literature I have read and the companies that I have consulted for have stopped at this phase—in fact, they have confused recognition with rewards. Employees often go away from a reward banquet feeling good for a brief time, or feeling that somewhere, something is missing in the picture. There are ways of giving this kind of appreciation that are more effective than others, and in the pages that follow, I will address some of these practical, proven suggestions and techniques.

Stage 3: Acknowledgment

Acknowledgment happens when a person feels "seen, heard, and understood." It's acknowledgment of who one is as a unique individual. Hopefully, all of us have had moments when we realize that someone "gets" who we are. They know that our artistic ability or our quick wit or our special brand of compassion is really what is important to us and what we feel makes us special. That person sometimes doesn't have to say a word or give us a citation. We just know that they know us—and that is enough. Unfortunately, it is a rare occurrence because recognition puts the person we are attempting to recognize at the center, not ourselves. I am not grateful for what you have done for me or my company or the division, I simply am acknowledging who *you* are. Sometimes this relationship takes place in a marriage—and that is great. Often, it occurs among friends who see us accomplish something they knew we had fear of and simply smile. It is part of my life's work (and this book is a part of that) to find ways for it to occur in the workplace and in organizations where people spend a great deal of their time, and therefore their lives. One of our greatest potentials as humans is to empower and acknowledge one another. The process of healing and growth is immensely quickened when another's belief in us is freely given.

A person feels recognized not simply for what's been accomplished, but for who he or she is as a unique individual. Appreciation that gets specific to behavior and then generalizes that behavior to a personal valued characteristic is getting closer to quality recognition that includes acknowledgment. This is the heart and center of true quality recognition. We'll talk more about it later.

Stage 4: Acceptance

Acceptance comes only when a person knows that not only what they do, but who they are makes a difference. Often, others become jealous or intimidated when they "get us"—when they realize the full strength of who we are, and as a result begin to undermine us or find ways to eliminate us because we are a perceived threat! This is hardly what I am speaking of. Unfortunately, this happens all too frequently in the workplace.

You may be skeptical and therefore asking whether or not true personal acceptance can in practice happen in corporations or if it is even consistent within a bottom-line, profit-oriented culture. You may be asking, how can we make this work and challenge ourselves to experience greater wholeness as human beings in the workplace? You may be reluctant to accept that new and breakthrough models can work, because up to now you have failed to believe they can and lack the practical "how-to's" necessary to apply the efforts and techniques that will make them work. You may also be asking, are we ready and are we willing to make the change? All of these questions will be dealt with in this book. It is my intent to help us all to reflect on the assumptions we have held about what is possible at work, and perhaps even at times, what is the function of work in our lives. I don't pretend to have all of the answers—I do have some. But in raising the consciousness of more people on this important topic, I KNOW collectively that the answers exist, when we focus on the right questions!

RECOGNITION: HOW TO GIVE IT

It is my intention that *Recognition: The Quality Way* will be a catalyst for companies and individuals to look at whether what they are currently calling recognition truly includes awareness, appreciation, acknowledgment, and acceptance.

In this book, I also begin to delineate how individuals go about looking for and getting these needs met. I address the efforts (and lack thereof!) that corporations have made in the recognition process. Remember—my thesis, based on my experience, is that IF corporations are recognizing employees at all, most are stopping at the appreciation phase. Sometimes they think they are recognizing employees by giving out "honors" on special occasions, but they have failed to be truly aware of the person on a day-to-day basis. None of the steps can be bypassed if quality recognition is to truly take hold in an organization.

As a basis for further study of the recognition process, I will take a look at popular theories of motivation and rely on some recent findings from business, neuro-linguistic programming, and the therapeutic models expressed through Virginia Satir as well as the Transformation Theory of adult learning, which discusses the way people change and the factors that motivate change. We'll also address how to foster the process. You will learn when and how to give yourself recognition and explore some unique ways of helping others feel recognized as well.

If you are unfamiliar with the literature on TQM, you'll find the brief summary of the movement helpful. You'll also find an analysis of what has already been written on the topic of recognition, especially such TQM gurus as Deming, Juran, Ishikawa, and Crosby. My intent is to help you to do "one-stop-shopping" and get all the information that has been written to date in one place. (Unfortunately, there has been little written to date—but much can be implied from other things that have been and are being said.)

Based on studies of differences in personality by people like Carl Jung, Isabel Myers, and Katherine Briggs as well as other popular models of personality or style differences (e.g., the VAK or visual, auditory, and kinesthetic model of NLP), I will highlight and underscore the importance of the individual and organizational recognition process. My focus is on how to customize a program so that it meets individual needs. Numerous examples from existing programs will be given to illustrate the point and you, the reader, will be led to answer questions about your own recognition needs and style.

Many companies must reevaluate the way they are organized to see if they are fostering the concept of teams while recognizing individual differences—a delicate balance. Teams are best composed of people with different skills and interests and NEED to use each others skills cooperatively for work to get done in the best quality fashion. Companies often sabotage team efforts by awarding bonuses to individual members at the expense of other members. One marketing department at a major communications company recently set a good example of this. Employees were called in to a meeting and told that 10% of their previous salary would now have to be earned as commissions. But, the commission pool was so large they had to prove that they did more than the other members of their team to deserve it! We'll see more of how companies (sometimes inadvertently) thwart that effort.

There is a major discrepancy in the issue of rewarding *results* only—especially those results that effect the bottom line—instead of focusing on the *process* and recognizing at that moment the specific behaviors and characteristics. Individuals get the idea that they are valuable only for what they produce, rather than for who they are and may conclude that they are being used and could easily be replaced. In the past few years, we have seen a great deal of emphasis on customer service. What TQM is aiming at is a culture of excellence where profit is a natural result of satisfied customers. Sometimes we forget the latter in pursuit of the former. We must focus more on employees as internal customers and realize that when their needs are met, the process goes smoother and profitable results are a natural consequence. You will find some practical means of recognizing individual and team effort while in process, not simply after a task is completed.

You will find a discussion of the idea of corporatewide programs of presenting company memorabilia, and then you will be given a taste of when and how these things can be effective in promoting a team idea—primarily after one already exists, not as a means of creating team spirit. To see how this is being done well, we'll study and model companies who have good programs in place. We'll visit with such leaders as Ben & Jerry, Mary Kay Cosmetics, Wal-Mart, and Southwest Airlines.

For the practical side of all of us, you'll find ideas that can be used NOW to get started. This is exactly what it says, a listing in a brainstorm-like fashion of ideas people have tried and used successfully without creating a total program. Although the emphasis of most of the book will be on the need to create programs from the top down, this information will be of help if you find yourself in a company whose TOP isn't really behind you or your programs. It is not optimal (what ever is?), however, these suggestions can be put in place without getting massive levels of approval or permission. Some are as simple (??) as learning to look someone directly in the eye while saying thank you for something specific.

RECOGNITION: HOW TO GET IT

Few of us come from ideal homes and have received the recognition that we deserve and therefore need to enhance our self-esteem. Although corporations are not here to serve as therapists for social ills, it would be remiss to leave out a chapter that addresses dysfunctional behavior patterns. Much has been written on the corporation as dysfunctional family. And so, I acknowledge what has been written in this arena and move on to more positive suggestions for how to get healthy recognition.

Do you know how to ask specifically for what you want and need to be recognized for? It's time to help end the mind-reading that so many believe "should" go on. As I teach, I know that I am learning to be clearer about the outcome I wish to achieve in all of my communications, verbal and written. As I ask for what I want, and ask the right person, I GET what I ask for! We can all use help in getting better at this. Clear communication certainly is a major part of achieving quality results.

You'll find some helpful hints on getting clearer about when to ask others and how and when to give yourself the recognition you want and deserve.

1

MOTIVATION

Have you ever given thought to what truly motivates you to do the things you do in life? What makes you get up day after day and keep on living? What makes one person go on to excel at a profession while another just gets by? What makes one person content in a job, while others in the same position seem so unhappy? All of us are motivated. We may not be motivated to do the things we truly *have* to do or should be doing or even the things we seem to *want* to do, but we are nonetheless continually motivated, even if it appears as if it is to do nothing.

I went to graduate school in New York City, and without judgment, I wondered each day as I passed the homeless on the streets why I was studying for a doctorate and why they were doing what they were doing—at the moment, at least. The motivating factors are many. It's not a simple question and answer sequence. But let me share with you some of the thoughts and studies I've done in pursuit of just such answers. Many of the comments in this chapter come from the formal and informal interviews that I have conducted over the past six years, in pursuit of an answer to this question.

Some would say that we are motivated to seek happiness, so we do what gives us pleasure at the moment. Some people have more of a future orientation and so are motivated by a pleasure that they know is forthcoming.

Fast food, microwaves, and credit cards that let us "buy now, pay later" have catered to the need for instant gratification. The proliferation of health clubs, for example, also attests to the fact that some people are willing to work now for a reward they will attain later. Some people choose to forego the chocolate cake for dessert tonight, knowing that they will be pleased next week or next month when that pair of pants fits better.

Others think we are motivated more to avoid pain than we are to gain pleasure. If the aerobics class or the chocolate cake were in a lion's den, few of us would even consider it! There is a lot of support for the old viewpoint, "No pain, no gain". People seem to change most only when it gets to be a HAVE TO! Witness how many people continue to smoke, overeat, drink, or have unsafe sex even though society loudly spells out the consequences.

We all seem to be conditioned by our upbringing and experience to value certain things more than others. And, we are all born with somewhat clearly delineated personality types—whatever model you may choose to view them through. It is a combination of our values and personality that determines our needs. Although we all need to sleep, for example, some people sleep more when they are anxious and some stop sleeping completely. Some have a need to have their homes in impeccable order and others only feel comfortable with all their things around them. At times we call it style or taste. We go into the homes or offices of our friends and we can tell a lot about them. There are vast differences between the sleek, clean lines of modern furniture and the French Country or Baroque styles that thrive on clutter. Given any group of individuals, they will differ vastly and yet on certain things they would be alike. I meet with a group of friends monthly for lunch. Our personalities are different, our tastes in food or clothing are different, and so are our needs for security, love, and communication. Yet, we seem to share so much in common. Are we more alike than different, or are we more different than alike? Uniqueness intrigues me.

What does all of this have to do with recognition? Do all people need recognition? Do we all need it equally or expressed in the same way? These are two very different questions. We all seem to be motivated by what we consider important in our lives, and what seems to be most important to us as humans is whatever makes us feel our own sense of importance. "The deepest urge in human nature," said John Dewey, "is the desire to be important." Motivating others is the art of finding out what makes them feel worthwhile, needed, wanted, and special. Recognition is the science of discovering what matters to people, and of letting people feel that they matter; that that are seen, heard, and understood by at least one other individual. Learning this art and science is the surest secret to success. It incorporates the ability to listen and to put another's interest before your own. It is what those in the field of communication call, developing the 'you' attitude. All advertisers and marketers know this truth. How effectively we put this into practice in our daily lives is the real test of our abilities as leaders and managers.

In her book, *The Possible Human* (J.P. Tarcher, 1982), Jean Houston tells a powerful story from her own life. Because it so poignantly expresses many of my ideas, I'll retell it here:

When Jean was 18 and a junior in college, she was president of the college drama society, a member of the student senate, winner of off-Broadway critics' awards for acting and directing, director of the class play, and had just turned down an offer to train for the Olympics in fencing. She was on top of a world that one day came to a crash. Three members of her family and a close friend all died suddenly. The scenery of the off-Broadway production fell on her head, and she was left almost blind. She lost her friends, her confidence, and her academic standing all within a period of a few months. She compared her life to that of Job's, she felt tragic and alone.

One day, after she had tentatively begun participating in class again, a young Swiss professor of religion, Dr. Jacob Taubes, stopped her on the way to the bus and told her that she had an interesting mind and that her reactions were important to him. She was startled by his acknowledgment.

"He attended to me," she said. "I existed for him in the realest of senses, and because I existed for him I began to exist for myself." Within several weeks, she regained her eyesight and her spirits, and became a fairly serious student, whereas before, as she put it, she had been, at best, a bright show-off.

What happened was that he acknowledged her when she most needed it. She was empowered in the midst of an experience that could have altered the direction of her life.

Recognition has the power to transform lives. We all need it! I have friends who say they don't need to be recognized. I also find that often when I meet someone and tell them that I speak and write on recognition, they tell me that they are "beyond that" and that they have come to be internally motivated and do not need the external recognition. Many people seem to confuse fame, prestige or status seeking, or even such motivators as achievement and power, with recognition. We all differ when it comes to our needs and the ways in which we want to receive external support and encouragement or affirmation. But what is common to us all is the need to know that we matter to someone outside of ourselves. Dale Carnegie, in *How to Win Friends and Influence People* (Simon & Schuster, 1936), puts it this way, "If you tell me how you get your feeling of importance, I'll tell you what you are. That determines your character. That is the most significant thing about you." Fame, for some, is what gives them their own sense of importance—it's one way of getting it—just one brand, one flavor. For some, prestige or power are their means. Others need to know that what they do and who they are serves others and contributes to the evolution of life on this planet. We all have our favorites. The bottom line is that we all need to have our sense of importance validated and we tend to do this by seeking recognition and sometimes even praise from others by one means or another. We cannot truly be fully who we are without relationships. We are defined, in a sense, by our relationships. The people who have loved us and accepted us have indeed created us. The masterful leader knows this to be true and works to know how to bring forth the best in others as a result.

To create a culture where quality comes first, it is important for organizational leaders to study, understand, and interpret human behavior. This must take precedence to studying and understanding how to interpret Pareto charts and other statistical tools. So many companies seem to have this in reverse order. Most of the change that is needed does not require technical or scientific skill, it requires psychological and social skills. Only when we truly come to know the people who work in these businesses and organizations and let them know that who and what they are makes a difference, will we experience the effects as a quality revolution. It is important that we understand motivation, the process and problems related to change and the way to ensure motivation and change through recognition.

MOTIVATION—WHAT IS IT?

Motivation is simply the reason we have for doing the things we do when and how we do them. People are motivated by such things as a love of life, a desire to succeed, fear of failure, the need for self-fulfillment or self-esteem. Often we are motivated by more unconscious factors that have become part of us through our tradition, our parents, or the rules of our church or government. Much of our motivation comes from our stereotypes of perfection. We are and we do what we believe is best for us—at all times. It may not appear best in someone else's eyes, or by someone else's standards, but each of us choose to do what we do because we believe it is in our best interest. Think about the reaction we have when we are told we did something wrong. Very often, our first impulse is to defend or justify ourselves. People even get seriously sick because, unconsciously at least, they believe it is the best way to get the attention they are craving. No one comes to work, for example, desiring to do a poor job on a particular day. A person may be more motivated to sleep, or to talk on the phone, or dawdle through the day's activities, but the initial set up is not to perform poorly.

Job performance is the result of motivation and ability. Ability includes training, education, equipment, simplicity of task, experience, and both inborn mental and physical capacity. Given all of these at their peak, a person still may not perform well on the job if motivation is not directed at the particular task. In 1983, the Public Agency Foundation surveyed 850 workers and found that 87% of those surveyed believed that if they worked harder, their employers would be the only ones to benefit. We've come a long way since 1983, with introduction of teams and participative management and employee ownership, but I wonder how many still believe that they are working for someone else's benefit? We obviously still have not learned the simple lesson of thinking first of others. "Do unto others as you would have them do unto you." This rule clearly works in life. Why does business seem to make itself exempt from what are universal truths?

Employee motivation is not something management does, rather it's a process that management fosters and allows to happen. People are always motivated. Leaders simply must provide an environment that fosters and supports their motivation. People only learn when they believe they have a need to know. It behooves us to learn what other people need! Max DePree of Herman Miller furniture store once said, "The common wisdom is that American managers have to learn to motivate people. Nonsense. Employees bring their own motivation. What people need from work is to be liberated, to be involved, to be accountable, and to reach for their potential. Leadership as the liberation of talent, rather than restraint by rule, is a common theme in all winning enterprises."

Motivational strategies abound in today's workplace. All executives are using some theory of motivation, whether they are aware of it or not. We all have basic assumptions about human nature, and our efforts at motivating ourselves and others are based on these assumptions. In *Iacocca: An Autobiography* (Bantam, 1986), Lee Iacocca tells of studying psychology and abnormal psychology as well as business and engineering. He asserts that these were the most valuable courses of his career because, by studying the fundamentals of human behavior, he learned how to answer the question, "What motivates that guy?" Let's look, therefore, at the theories that have shaped our own understanding and what insights they give us into quality recognition.

B.F. Skinner and Behavioral Science

Although Skinner primarily studied animal behavior, much of the work of behavioral science can be equally applied to humans as well. Some of the major points of behavioral science as it relates to quality recognition include:

- Behavior is shaped almost exclusively by the effects of an outside stimulus being applied, as well as by both positive and negative reinforcement.

- Actions that are reinforced or rewarded tend to be repeated more frequently under the same or similar conditions.

- Reinforcement is most effective when it is timed correctly—that is, when it occurs during or immediately upon the conclusion of the behavior that one wants to affect.

Skinner also concluded that animals rewarded for good behavior learn far more rapidly and retain what they learn far more effectively than animals punished for bad behavior. We can observe this in action with children. When they get attention by crying, they learn to cry! When we continually reward good behavior instead of punishing wrong behavior, the good behavior multiplies. Many parents and teachers have found that if they stop yelling and instead watch for behavior that they like—and reward it with a hug or a word of praise—miracles seem to happen.

I remember a story I read years ago from a book called *Don't Shoot the Dog* (Simon & Schuster, 1984) by Karen Pryor. She tells of a teacher who had habitually harangued an art class over their failure to complete homework. One bright student, tired of being constantly scolded, suggested that the teacher begin to praise those who did do the work rather than hassle those who didn't. In about three weeks, the teacher found that the homework turn-in ratio had almost doubled.

Positive reinforcement works especially well for teenagers and adults! I remember a trick I used to use to keep myself studying when I wanted to be elsewhere. For each chapter I completed or each theorem I memorized, I allowed myself some small reward. Sometimes, it was as simple as a walk around the block. Some of my adult students have set rewards for themselves when they finish their degree. For many, it's plans of an exotic vacation, or a large purchase they've been promising themselves. We learn this reward behavior early on, and advertisers reinforce it throughout our lives, such as McDonald's "You deserve a break today . . ."

Psychologists have noted that what seem to be variant behaviors in humans can actually be traced to decisions that the unconscious mind made at an early age about what behaviors would be repeated based on perceived rewards. This is true, for example, in the case of a pathological liar, who learns to lie initially to please someone and then continues to lie as a habit. Positive behaviors develop the same way. We do whatever we perceive that we need to, either to avoid pain or to increase pleasure. One of the interesting findings of behavioral science that is relevant to our study of recognition is that intermittent rather than continuous reinforcement actually increases response. Translated, this simply means that when rewards are given too often, the motivation diminishes. Although a vacation after every completed semester sounds good, it would actually diminish the effect of this particular motivator. This is why a pay check is not enough of a motivator on a job. It is something that people come to expect. We seem to like the surprise factor in motivation. At Sea World, entire shows are run in which the animals never know what behavior will be reinforced next and by what means. The whales, for example, may be given fish, or stroked and scratched, or even given audience applause. The surprises seem to be what challenges the performers.

When we receive praise, recognition, or an increase in pay that is unexpected, it is a greater motivator than when we know something is coming. Think about this in terms of what Ken Blanchard, in his *One Minute Manager* (Morrow, 1990), talks about as "catching people doing something right." Blanchard's idea is to help employees set out clear goals and understand what they are accountable for. Expectations and standards of good performance are clearly laid out, but then employees are given clear, immediate, consistent, and specific feedback at various times. If we simply set out a program of rewards, and everyone knows when they are forthcoming, they have less effect than the "instant" rewards that come unexpectedly when someone simply praises you for a job well done at the moment. It's like betting on a racehorse or standing at a Las Vegas slot machine. We seem to thrive on the possibilities of a large payoff. Think about a dancer or any performer. It is not the debriefing in the dressing room that really supports good performance, but the "Yes" and "Move now" comments that are given at the moment the performance occurs that really reinforces the desired behavior. Think about the reinforcement we give athletes when a touchdown or run is scored. They get instant feedback from the roar of the crowd, and from their teammates.

So, we learn that in addition to being sporadic, the timing of our reinforcement is very important as well. When reinforcement comes too late, it may serve to have the opposite effect. Have you ever received a compliment such as, "You looked great yesterday." This causes you to wonder what's wrong with the way you look today!

Recognition cannot be a "program" you put in as part of a move towards total quality—it must become a way of life, part of the "on-the-job" training that we give to employees. *Recognition: The Quality Way* is part and parcel of the culture of an organization. It's not something we do, but someone we are! It is the way people are treated on a daily basis, not just what happens at the end of the month, the quarter, or the year. People need to be noticed.

People need frequent, sporadic, yet continuous feedback about *progress* throughout the work year, not just at reward time. Random, unpredictable reinforcement is far more effective than a constant, predictable schedule. And timing, as in life, is everything!

Maslow and the Hierarchy of Needs

Abraham Maslow is perhaps the most cited of all motivational theorists. His major premise is that people are motivated to satisfy needs and that these needs can be arranged in a hierarchy. We can look at the various levels of his hierarchy to discuss how to be certain that an employee's needs are being met so that recognition can be effective.

Level 1

Physiological needs are those that are essential to survival. In this list, Maslow includes food, water, rest, and sex. Employees' physiological needs are met by the environments in which they interact and by the amount of time arranged for such things as breaks, meals, and vacations. Some organizations fail to recognize even these basic needs. Their programs of recognition would obviously need to start here. It makes no sense to give out plaques and trophies at a ceremony once a year, if during a normal workday, an employee is forced to work in extreme heat or to work excessive hours.

I worked in an office once where we didn't have enough chairs and desks for all employees. The management assumed that because many of us were frequently on the road, we didn't need to have our own space and could share an office with five or six others. I'm talking about a space that was originally meant for one—or at most two! The days that we were all in the office, people would take turns sitting on the chairs, or on the windowsills. Needless to say, productivity was certainly lowered considerably.

Unfortunately, this situation is not over-exaggerated nor rare. Many of the companies we worked with, who were busy filling out forms to compete for quality awards, were doing so under conditions that certainly don't tell an employee that he or she is worth having around. When a company says, "we can't afford space for you", they are in essence saying, "you really don't matter, after all. But, where are those numbers???"

Unkempt environments or places where boxes crowd out people, or offices in basements with clanging pipes and no windows to see the weather outside are also common in many places. Fortunately, there are equally as many where there are brightly colored walls and pictures as well as well-lit, well-ventilated rooms that say, we're glad you're here. I used to love to visit places like General Foods in White Plains, New York where there were original quilts hanging on the walls and spotless mirrors over everything. You can bet their employees always looked their best. They seemed to work that way too. Psychologists have taught us that even color schemes affect our moods. I've seen many good examples of this in my travels. There are many exceptional architectural wonders where floors and rugs are brightly color-coded and where bubbling fountains speak of life. Quality products and services have a better chance of being produced in quality environments.

Level 2

Safety and security needs include the need for protection against physical and psychological threats in the environment and an assurance that these needs will be met in the future. Company benefit packages and job security fall into this category. If people are without proper health and life insurance, or are living under the threat of layoffs, certificates and awards become meaningless. True recognition must include what we've come to see as basic.

Unfortunately, many organizations have elaborate reward and recognition systems and yet employees live under such constant threats as sexual harassment or job extinction. Or, with the daily barbs of a boss who lacks common kindness or manners. Or, under bullies who continually emit threats. Before we can add positive behaviors, we must get rid of the negative contradictions. People must feel that their jobs are secure and that their psychological safety is insured as well.

Level 3

Social needs include a sense of belonging, association, affiliation, and acceptance by others, including the need for social interaction and for affection and support. These personal needs are even more important than being told that you succeeded in a job task. We all need to feel as if we matter, as if who we are and what we do makes a difference.

A true understanding of total quality includes the notion of shared responsibility. For quality programs to work, the members must feel a sense of ownership not only for their specific task, but also for the organization as a whole. A basic human need is to feel that we are a part of something bigger than ourselves.

I recently had a rather frustrating experience attempting to buy a car that I had previously leased. The company I was doing business with was located across the country, so all of our transactions had to be by phone. The first person who called me quoted figures and dates and assured me that he was the person who could give me the best deal, because he was the manager. A few weeks later, when no contract appeared to be forthcoming, I called again and spoke to someone who gave me completely different figures. He claimed to be the owner's son, and yet all during the conversation, he spoke of the company as "they" whenever he wanted to suggest that he couldn't do what I was asking. He was either using a common cop-out, or was a classic example of "victimization." Although I firmly believe that as human beings we are responsible for our own actions and thoughts, and only victims by choice, when someone talks about the place they work as an entity apart from themselves, that is a clear indication that something is amiss in the area of these third-level needs. We'll talk at length about this later.

Level 4

This level encompasses the need for self-respect and esteem from others. We all have a need for both intrinsic and extrinsic motivation. Studies have proven that babies who live without touch eventually die. Psychological touch here is as important as physical touch. Although I will later advocate for not seeking recognition as a way of getting it, it is our responsibility as a society to take care of one another's needs in this regard. It may be psychologically unhealthy to seek ALL sense of self outside of yourself, but to get none is equally unhealthy. Our need for outside recognition is so strong that often people resort to negative behavior just so someone will notice them. At the heart of most problem behavior is simply a need and desire to be seen. It's time we come to realize how basic a need it is to get outside acknowledgment of who we are and what we do. It's close to the need for survival.

Managers working from this fuller assumption about the nature of the human being recognize talent and reward outstanding contribution while meeting the objectives of the organization. They know that people have needs that are psychological as well as physical and social, and begin to make better use of talents, creativity, and imagination.

They begin to delegate and rally people around campaigns. They begin to be concerned about quality of life and good work environments so that people can work to their potential for the good of the environment.

Level 5

Self-actualization is the opportunity to fulfill one's potential and grow more clearly into the unique expression that each of us was meant to be. Ira Progoff, in his book and seminar *At a Journal Workshop* (J.P. Tarcher, 1992), speaks of "asking our lives what they wish to become" and then being all we can. More and more individuals have become aware of this need for full self-expression and more and more organizations are becoming aware of the need to address issues of personal growth. These needs are no longer left up to the individual. Total quality organizations can only happen when the individual members who make up the organization are fully functioning. We spend so much of our lives working in organizations. Organizations, therefore, have a responsibility to help us meet these higher needs.

What the quality movement has done is raised awareness of these higher level needs. We are acknowledging the importance of having a vision or mission, of working and living according to value, of leadership with principle. We are witnessing a spiritual awakening of the organization. We have come to realize that people are not only physical, social, and psychological, but that they are by nature, spiritual. What we are noticing in the literature is a greater movement toward organizations becoming aware of addressing the esteem and self-actualization needs of their members. There is a drive in all of us for meaning greater than ourselves. People want to contribute to the accomplishment of something that is worthwhile and bigger than they are alone. It is not a matter of simply using talents and creativity more fully, it is doing things that bring them to a higher, truer sense of the Self.

When we begin to talk about empowerment, we are speaking of more than allowing people to collaborate and participate in someone else's ideal. We are inviting people into a realm where they are inspired and uplifted to live lives congruent with the larger beliefs and values that truly yield dramatic results. With works such as Steven Covey's *Principled-Centered Leadership* (Summit, 1991), we've replaced goal setting with an understanding of working according to values and principle. This necessitates managers finding ways to allow employees freedom to make their own work challenging and fulfilling. People want to take pride in their work and must know that what they do is appreciated. Routine, repetitive tasks can be automated to free the person from behind the machine. Decision-making that incorporates the ideas of all MUST be more effective than those that had been unilateral.

We can imagine business itself as a person who has to go through stages and has an increasingly complex hierarchy of needs. In childhood, there is a great deal of concentration on physical needs. As children, we learn to walk, to talk, and get potty trained. By the time we reach adolescence, we come to see the social nature of our being and it is during this time that we experience the greatest pull of peer pressure and belonging urges. As we grow to adulthood, we become aware of ourselves as psychological beings as well. We begin to question our career goals and our life-mate choices. True growth in adulthood demands self-direction. When we reach maturity, we grasp the essential nature of life as something beyond our physical existence and we realize that we have a control over and responsibility for our own destiny.

As our organizations evolve, we need to find more and more ways to allow for personal control in everyday work.

Civilization is coming to a consciousness of responsibility. More and more people are recognizing and desiring to live by choice rather than victimization or coercion. Managers and true leaders must rid themselves of outdated assumptions and simplify their organizations so that they can experience the full benefit of effective, free workers. Before we can set up the "how to's," we need to come to a full awakening of the why. Motivating people to high-level performance demands recognizing the individual as well as the organization. It takes an open mind to note that when individual goals and capabilities are stretched to their maximum, and when people are truly feeling satisfied and fulfilled in their work life, that work will benefit and organizational needs will be met as well. We've been doing things in reverse order for so long that this will take a real paradigm shift. It takes a spiritual view to accept the truth that human beings, and all of life, is essentially one and good. Therefore, what is good for the individual, what serves his or her needs, actually serves the needs of the collective good as well.

Recognition: The Quality Way focuses on those needs. We have finally come to realize that the drive and desire to be loved, to be appreciated, and to feel like we matter to someone are not added extras anymore. It is an idea whose time has come. As a people, we have "progressed." Our companies must learn to keep up with the times or perish. Survival in a global economy no longer is akin to personal survival—it is essential now that we become aware of helping people achieve their highest potential and become all that they can become. Maslow's hierarchy has been leveled along with the structures of our organizations. We have discovered that hierarchical systems are antiquated. Self-directed work-teams require self-actualized people—or at least those on their way—and using Maslow's theory, that means at least high on the self-esteem/self-actualization list with needs for recognition being well met!

Douglas Hall and Age Theory

Several motivation theories, like Maslow's, are stage dependent. Others, like that of Douglas Hall, relate more directly to a person's chronological age. Hall believes that motivation is based on needs, but these needs are entirely dependant on age, which usually relates to the stage one is at in one's career. A person in their early career is seeking advancement, friendships, and money, developing skills and recognition in the traditional sense. Employees under the age of 30 often rank "good wages" as first in an order of what is important on a job, while people over 50 are more concerned with "interesting work."

For the majority of the workers between the ages of 40 and 55, the needs switch to achievement, independence, ability utilization, power and prestige, and self-actualization. Although not all people follow a set pattern, many people in this age group will tell you that to be recognized in some instances means to be left alone—to be trusted to do one's work in the best possible way. Adulthood is a quest for self-direction and the more one becomes self-directed, the more important attempts at recognition acknowledge this thrust.

The way you recognize a 20-year old, then, would clearly be different from the way you recognize someone who is approaching 40 or 50. In the earlier stages, money, titles, and opportunity for training are ways to keep an employee satisfied. So, bonuses mean more when a person is building a family and saving for the future. As a person matures, the sense of having accomplished something and the acknowledgment of expertise in a given area are more important things to notice. They usually are more sensitive to issues of personal growth as well, and so would value someone noticing their personal traits like honesty, integrity, and perseverance. To become a master motivator, one must learn to be sensitive to what these psychologists have taught us about differences. Though all people in a given age group are not necessarily alike, beginning to recognize age factors in motivation is at least a place to start.

This whole concept of recognizing the different ways different age groups want to be motivated leaves wide open the question of rewarding people as teams. Teams are usually comprised of people from varying backgrounds as well as varying age groups. If our needs are different at different ages, wouldn't it stand to reason that our rewards should be different as well? How are we doing that now?

Frederick Herzberg and Motivators

Herzberg added a new twist to the age/stage theories. He asserted that we cannot begin to motivate someone until the things that dissatisfy that person have been removed. Salary, working conditions, and supervision are not motivators even when they are met. They simply help to keep a person from being dissatisfied. Dissatisfiers can also include company policy, poor interpersonal relations, and job security. Meeting lower-level needs of employees is not motivating, but can be demotivating when not met. It is only when we begin to meet someone's higher-level needs that motivation truly kicks in.

No recognition or other form of motivation can compensate for pay that is under expectation. Many people that I have interviewed complained about company parties. They were suggesting quite clearly that they were tired of hearing that the company couldn't afford to pay them better wages but somehow seemed to have money in the budget for these "trivialities" or "extravagances." One software vendor has employees working in such cramped quarters, but pays extraordinary bonuses to people for their longevity in sticking it out. Extra bonuses seem ludicrous when day-to-day living is uncomfortable at best! Company picnics that are meant to improve morale, when your best friend has been laid off the week before, just don't work.

Try talking to anyone in the defense industry today about motivation. When job security is at stake and no one knows who is the next to get the ax, no technique, gimmick, or even sincere effort will motivate. Even when all the basic needs of adequate salary, fair supervision, job security, and sufficient working conditions have been met, the best that can be said is that people will not be dissatisfied. That still doesn't spell motivation.

Motivation factors must be tied to the work itself. They are directly related to a sense of achievement and to a feeling of recognition. When these are met, the individual feels satisfied (i.e., is motivated). Herzberg's studies show that the motivators that will enhance satisfaction after dissatisfiers are overcome are achievement, recognition, responsibility, growth opportunity, and the work itself. These factors can be thought of as job enrichers.

Government engineers that I spoke to cited that they get a charge "just by doing the job." Their reward seems to result directly from performing their tasks. "When the job itself includes challenge and opportunity for achievement and an opportunity to control the pace and outcome, then success is a given." I don't think these engineers are alone in this.

Back in 1968, Herzberg was advocating giving the employee more control, allowing greater job freedom, and granting additional authority. Twenty-five years later, we are hearing the same cry. Herzberg also recommended that this be an ongoing process and not just a one-time proposition. He saw that intrinsic motivation only works when a person feels that someone recognizes their ability and need to work on tasks of increasing difficulty, to take ownership for a total process—not just add a piece—and to be given the tools, training, and time needed to become an expert. A sense of achievement and recognition for a job well-done, a greater sense of responsibility, a genuine sense that the company or organization provides opportunity for personal and professional growth, and work itself that uses a person's talents and abilities are all parts of *Recognition: The Quality Way.* We would do well to take Herzberg's advice to heart today.

Management by Objectives (MBO)

One way many organizations have handled individual differences was through the use of a method introduced in the 1950s by Peter Drucker. Drucker's idea centered around goal setting as an optimal way for management to ensure that organizational objectives were met. He introduced the idea of a manager's letter. It suggests that subordinates prepare some form of a written outline that includes desired results and guidelines as well as the resources needed, and the lines of accountability. This method also serves as a way of recognizing individual differences and incentives because each person, in theory at least, sets his or her own work goals in relation to the ones that have been set down by upper management. The method centers around setting long- and short-term goals as well as action plans to determine how these goals were to be met. Everything is mapped out and planned in advance and all tasks are thus assigned. The assumption is that employees who are part of the planning of their goals and action steps will take greater responsibility for self-motivation to get these done. Finally, employee reviews and evaluations are done to see if the person meets their objectives.

From my study of adult education and my work with corporate clients, I have learned that setting objectives is always tenuous at best. Life does not allow us to predetermine the lessons it hands us. Although general guidelines and a sense of direction are important, to specifically define all the objectives and goals a person must meet for a year or six months at a time can actually stifle initiative and growth. It doesn't allow the person the flexibility to change that is needed in our fast-paced technological society. There must be a healthy balance between setting goals and keeping our eyes open to constant change. We are so accustomed to the quick-fix, fast temporary relief, bottom-line mentality. Goals are important in life, but they have a tendency to have us live in the future rather than in the present moment. In the long run, this seems to be more destructive to both the individual and to society.

Very often, we sacrifice the present as we work hard toward accomplishing some goal, only to find when we have reached it that it wasn't what we really wanted or it wasn't the issue that really needed to be addressed. Here's where moving toward a more spiritually based paradigm of management can be very helpful. True masters in any arena know that life is essentially a goalless process. It is not really a goal or a destination that we seek, it is simply a process or journey that we are on. When we recognize it, we will realize that the true goal is what the total quality movement calls continuous improvement and what others are calling lifelong learning. To learn is to change. The process we really need to be involved in then, is learning how to learn.

SOME NEWER MODELS OF MOTIVATION

If we look at Peter Senge's model of the Learning Organization as defined in *The Fifth Discipline* (Doubleday, 1990), we will note that looking at individual departments and compartmentalized goals and objectives eliminates systems thinking. People begin to see their own piece of the pie to the exclusion of how what they are doing effects every other person, product, and action in the organization. Strict goal setting and evaluation based on the goals set stifles innovation and creativity. In a total quality approach, it is essential that goals be continually reexamined and revamped for continuous process improvement. Goal setting, by its very nature, tells us that we know what the end is. A spiritual approach encompasses a systems view. When Steven Covey, in The *Seven Habits of Highly Effective People* (Simon and Schuster, 1990) says, "Begin with the end in mind," he is talking about the value or principle behind what we are doing, not a rigid set of rules to follow. When we allow ourselves to be in process, we begin to learn about learning itself. When we get comfortable being in a learning mode, rather than being "at the bottom-line" conclusion mode, then we will be on the road to quality.

MBO requires massive paperwork and time and people often wind up trying to make "the end justify the means." What would happen if we truly moved toward a quality culture, where the process became the end and goals were not set in concrete but allowed to be fluid and changing?

People do seem to be motivated by goals. So, what am I saying? When our society was at the lower end of Maslow's need hierarchy, people needed goals to get their material needs met. When you are in survival, or your safety is threatened, it is important to keep a very narrow focus. Simply get the job done. At earlier ages and lower levels of need fulfillment, goal setting seems essential.

I've noticed that all the "success" teachers of the world teach goal setting. They have you write down the things you want and the ways you are going to get them. And, it works when we have specific goals. But when we open ourselves to the notion of continuous improvement, we move to a realm beyond the measurable and concrete. If we look at the "spiritual" teachers, we find that they teach "surrender" and "allowing" rather than just "making" things happen. Business itself seems to be moving to this higher level of existence and so, the things that worked to motivate us, to create the products and companies and organizations we wanted when business was in its adolescence, no longer meet the needs as it grows to adulthood. Surrender in business means to keep open to the continual present moment and alert for newer, better ways of improving what is being done. It implies being present in the relationship we are in with our boss, vendor, or peer. The quality of our relationships always improve when we meet people where they currently are, rather than where they were or where we would like them to be. Recognition of a person requires that I see where they are right now. We can learn from the Zen Masters to approach relationships and everything in life with what they call the "beginners mind." When we allow ourselves to realize that we don't know all the answers, we open ourselves to newness at every moment. No person is the same as they were yesterday. Today's experience has changed them. This attitude would keep us continually improving. The attitude that locks a person, or a system, or a product where it always has been, is the very antithesis of a quality approach.

THE TOTAL QUALITY MODEL
OF MOTIVATION

The total quality movement has the potential to teach us to live with the ambiguity and the dichotomy necessary to surrender and to have goals at the same time, IF it is seen in its totality. Stage one in a quality improvement process usually concentrates on goal setting. Statistical process control (SPC) and process improvement methods are among its tools. If we are to move to stage two and really see the transformation of organizations, we must include a vision that moves to the future by living more fully in the present. This type of vision recognizes the uniqueness of the individual and the power that we have when we utilize each person at his or her full potential. We create a synergy, a constantly changing, evolving environment moving towards its own fulfillment. This can be a frightening thought to those who seek to control and direct the future! To open ourselves to what the quality movement truly has to offer, we must be willing to change continuously at a pace that is faster than we have ever experienced. When we truly empower the masses, there is no telling what the energy released might do!

2

How People Change

It is a relatively simple thing to add new knowledge in our lives and experience change as a result. It is much more difficult to change someone's attitude or behavior. Managers must understand motivation so that they can understand why people do the things they do. To be effective leaders, they also must understand how to influence others to change.

Over the years, I have come to know, experience, and test the truth that we change more by love than correction. How one feels about changing often affects whether or not they will. I worked with someone once who had poor hygiene habits and everyone in our office tried to find ways to tell her. Her hair was unkempt and her clothing often was covered with stains. She was an exceptional worker, but it was an embarrassment when she represented the company before clients, which she often did. Because I worked closely with her, I began to experiment with this idea about how people change. Whenever she washed her hair, I would comment that it looked exceptionally nice that day and asked what she did differently. When she wore a dress or suit that fit properly and had no stains, I'd compliment her frequently during the day. After a while we all began to notice that whenever she and I were out together, she'd wear the clothes I "liked" and her hair was clean and combed. Over time, this became the rule rather than the exception.

What would it have done if we had told her outright that she had to change? Perhaps we would have lost a valuable employee and who knows if she would have truly understood. At the very least, she may have resented it and tried to defy me. She really didn't seem to notice before the compliments. What's that saying about catching more flies with honey? I think it applies here.

It may seem contradictory, but the best motivation to change is to believe that we are absolutely perfect as we are. As motivators of others, we must first know that where we are is perfect! That can be a very hard thing to learn, but it is the only way that true change occurs. Change comes best when you first accept and love *who* you are exactly *as* you are. I heard someone recently reprimanding his staff, by saying "You've got to change this and you've got to change that," but the staff backed off from everything that this person said. People change most when they experience being loved and being accepted exactly as they are . . . then they want to change. But if they "have" to change . . . watch out!

LESSONS FROM SPORTS

There is increasing evidence to support this type of positive management. In his book *Turning the Thing Around* (Hyperion, 1993), Jimmy Johnson talks about the way he motivated the Dallas Cowboys, transforming them from a team with a 1–15 record into Superbowl champions. He uses the positive feedback approach, acknowledging that the brain doesn't know the difference between positive and negative messages and in fact ignores the negative. If he were to tell his players, "Don't fumble," sure enough their mind would record "fumble" and they would do exactly that. He tried never to plant a negative seed. Instead, he would say to the running back, "Protect the ball." He suggests that the only way to motivate, coach, or manage is to make the players feel good about themselves. When he was strong and positive about high expectations, the players got the message and lived up to the expectations.

And old truism says, "Treat people as they are, and they will remain as they are. Treat people as if they were what they could be and should be, and they will become what they could be and should be." George Bernard Shaw made this famous in *Pygmalion* and it is one of the most repeated themes on Broadway. It's basically the psychology of the self-fulfilling prophecy.

Johnson's method worked because of his consistency. He treats even the rookies with profound respect and expectation. He's been heard to say, "Hey (first name), I saw you doing some really good things out there today. We think you can play here. We like you." Of course, sincerity is an important part of positive treatment. The only thing worse than a coach or CEO who doesn't care about people is one who pretends to care. Johnson cares. He doesn't always give positive reinforcement. The psychology of learning has shown that the most effective teaching method combines reinforcement with punishment as long as the reinforcement is at about 90%. When punishment or a reprimand is given to someone who is reinforced most of the time, that word is truly heard and absorbed. If someone is continually giving negative reinforcement, eventually their voice gets tuned out. Johnson acknowledges the individual while reinforcing the team. When asked if any of his players ever reach such a status or income level that they no longer need a pat on the back, he says boldly, "That's all bull. EVERYBODY needs positive reinforcements. And EVERYBODY wants to win. And, no matter the salary, players can be bonded with one another and care about one another as a team, if they're treated the right way."

When we truly care about another person, we don't try to remake them into an image of ourselves. The most effective changes take place when there is no resistance. When you force something, it doesn't work. When you allow it, it happens. Life is not really about making things happen—they happen anyway. We simply learn to let them be. We waste more energy on force and resistance.

The now popular 12-step programs have said it simply. Change is the end of a long process. First you must be able to observe what it is that you are doing that needs to be changed. Then, you become aware of the habit or forces that keep you entrenched in the same behavior. But, before you actually can make the change, you must accept yourself as you are, where you are, doing exactly what you are doing. It seems to be a universal truth that what we resist, persists. When we decide to accept what is, change is free to happen.

So, our task as managers/motivators in attempting to understand and celebrate differences is to accept people as they are. It is not our role in life to change anyone, or to make them "shape up". That very attitude forces people to resist. If people are truly our most important resource, our most important role is to support them.

Many adults today are struggling to recover and are focusing their lives on understanding and healing what has happened to them during their childhood. Authority figures have often done a whole lot of damage and those in authority must be certain not to continue to pass that damage on. This is not said to blame, but once again to observe the reality that exists. Most of us carry some scars from our experiences with authority, so to be in that position now means that you have the opportunity to help yourself and others overcome some of the things you, and the people you are leading, have gone through in their past. Every one of us could tell war stories about what happened in the past. It is amazing the kind of memories that we store. So it is with the employees who come to you. I am not suggesting that our role be only as "psychologists," but we must be "healers" as well! We are no longer managing machines; we are no longer managing processes; we are beginning to realize that managers who once simply worked to accomplish organizational goals must now become leaders who recognize the true source of productivity—people.

We send messages to people about their worth, and it affects them constantly. As leaders and change agents, we are in very important roles. We can have a tremendous effect on the self-esteem of the people we are leading. We can help people feel differently about themselves if we appreciate differences and are aware of what we say and do and how we say and do it. Our giving or withholding recognition can have a powerful impact on someone's self-view. When people begin to believe in themselves, and feel as if they are recognized and accepted, they begin to believe they can master an impossible task and much greater productivity occurs.

A technical trainer for a software vendor was getting the highest ratings they ever had in the company after only a month of knowing the product. Some of the heavy tech people in the company who had been teaching for years were frustrated by that. One guy came out and said, "They just like you more than they like me . . . that doesn't mean a thing!" And the trainer thought, "Isn't that interesting, I'm getting better ratings not because I know more, but because people like me. People don't like him. He comes across as intimidating and unfriendly, even though he really knows his subject." Hearing this interaction made me think. I observed that in my own life experience, I have learned most from people that I liked the most.

This reflection led me to do some research to find out who others best learn from. Think now about from whom you have learned in your life. I guarantee that it is people that you have liked and respected. This is especially true in grade school. Sometimes we remember teachers later as ones we liked—because they disciplined us! I am not saying that the best teachers are the ones who are naturally sweet and loving and kind. There were teachers we can all remember liking who were very tough. They knew how to make us toe the mark, but they did it with respect and gentleness and real love. There are some teachers who pride themselves on giving the minimum of praise. When this tactic seems to work, it is through a principle based on scarcity rather than abundance. When praise is scarce, even a brief nod or a grudging approval is taken to be highly rewarding. But even the praise-stingy teacher must in some way show respect for the student to get long-term positive results. The best teachers generally strive to point out what the student is doing right at least as frequently as what he or she is doing wrong. I know those are the people I really learned from and they are the ones that come to mind as I think of those outstanding teachers I have known and modeled.

Sports models continually teach us this. John Wooden, UCLA coach and perhaps the greatest basketball mentor of all time, managed to do this throughout his long winning career. Wooden claimed to have maintained a balanced ratio between reinforcement and correction. His players knew he respected them. The greats seem to know how to balance praise and correction when it is needed. Perhaps we can learn from these people still!

The best change agents are people who listen, accept, and model appropriate change behavior, rather than the ones who either tell you what's wrong or tell you nothing at all. Business can do well to learn from the tradition of sports as well as from some renowned change therapists.

VIRGINIA SATIR—A THERAPY MODEL

One of the most famous family therapists, Virginia Satir, gave us an interesting change model. She defines change first of all as "any wound to the system." The system begins in a stable state. It does not matter if the change is perceived as good (e.g., a promotion, a raise, or a new job) or bad (e.g., being terminated or lowering a quota). The fact is, we react to any change in the same manner. When the system is stable, people know what to expect. Everything is familiar and in balance. In this stage, the individual (or organization) knows how the world works and feels competent in using the rules. When A happens, they know they can expect B. People feel like they have control over their destiny. At this stage, people have a good sense of security, knowing that their basic needs will be met.

The change enters as a foreign element almost always introduced from the outside. This is the initiating factor, such as an upturn or downturn in business, a promotion or getting fired, starting a new job, or retiring. It is anything that changes the status quo. Change is always stressful even if it is a positive change. And, initially, most people try to ignore or expel it.

The two most common reactions to change are rejection and denial. Rejection is active and denial is passive. Rejection or resistance occurs when the individual or group acknowledge that the change is here and do everything that they know how to work against it happening. There is a strong desire to keep things the way they are, even if they weren't happy that way. Denial takes place when the rules have changed and there is confusion, but people are unaware that a change has taken place. This is always the result of a lack of knowledge or information. Many changes take place when the financial situation of a company changes. Companies that have closed books often fall prey to this denial stage. In this instance, ignorance is never bliss.

Both ignoring or trying to expel a change eventually lead to chaos because the system has been upset. There is a clear loss of congruence. The old predictions no longer work; old expectations are no longer being fulfilled. People no longer know how to behave. The rules are changed and cannot be changed back. Chaos refers to the feelings of despair illustrated with comments (voiced or unvoiced) such as: "I don't know how to do this"; "I am afraid of making mistakes and looking stupid"; "I might lose my job"; or "What if I can't get another job? I'll lose my house."

Self-image is challenged by the new situation. There is a vicious cycle that starts when people become unsure of themselves, become increasingly prone to making more mistakes and then as a result continue on a downward spiral of losing confidence. It is a risky time, when nothing seems sure. But it can also be an exhilarating time when new rules, new structures, and new organizations can be created. New opportunities have a fighting chance to emerge only after we have become comfortable in the chaos.

With the ever-changing environment of a total quality organization—a true learning organization—we need to do just that. Once we label the feelings of confusion that occur, and are able to admit and honor those feelings, then and only then will we have begun to be masters of the change process. And change is what the total quality movement is all about.

Eventually, when people begin to see new possibilities, a feeling of rebirth starts to set in. People start to practice new habits. There is a tremendous sense of power as they start learning the way the "new" world works. They start to feel competent and sure of themselves again. Every change, even the very worst, allows them to look at the world differently. Change creates new opportunities that were not available before. It allows for growth and the opportunity to increasingly become more than they were before.

Once we learn the new rules and the unfamiliar becomes the familiar again, in cyclical fashion, we are now back to the status quo. Of course, at this point, we can be certain that a new foreign element will come along and we'll be back in the cycle again.

In summary, Satir's change model includes six major stages:

1. Status quo.

2. Foreign element is introduced.

3. Denial—rejection.

4. Chaos.

5. Integration.

6. New status quo.

Any change can be viewed as a death, an ending of something we may have liked or not. What can we learn as change agents from this model about how we go about helping a person through the change process? It demands first that we be open about the fact that there is a process of change going on. We must make clear statements about where we are and where we need to be. So much can be said about the process of communication. A recognition program in some organizations must start with a radical change—openness in communication.

Next, it is important to acknowledge all of the people who the change will effect. Be specific about when it will take place and why it is necessary. Make clear what will change and what will not. What are the benefits? What will be the impact? In other words, be honest. The effect of this honesty upon the employee will be for him or her to feel like someone is at least aware of what is happening. When was the last time you observed your role as a change agent and actually acknowledged the process that your staff was going through in making a change— whether it be a complete company restructuring or a change in a small operations procedure?

If companies are honest about the move to a total quality approach to management, they must undergo major paradigm shifts and in most cases, complete culture changes. We need to learn as much as possible about how to be agents of change, or we may become part of the resistance. Change is happening all around us. To acknowledge that change is having an effect on people is one way of recognizing them. Whether a company is "rightsizing," or growing more quickly than they can handle, the problem of overworked employees remains the same. Most of the people I interviewed said that they were more than willing to work overtime or do the job of two or more, IF someone at least let them know they were aware that they were going above and beyond the call of duty. Simply saying, "I realize we are asking a great deal of you at this time, and we really appreciate the extra effort and time you have had to put in" can make the difference in whether or not someone feels recognized. At least you are acknowledging that this is a difficult thing. People are not unwilling to work, or even to pitch in and do more than their share when necessary, but they do need to know that someone notices. Of course, this has to be a temporary situation or like reinforcement—too much of this kind of pat on the back wears thin after awhile. The key is being congruent.

At the heart of Satir's theory is this notion of congruence. We are congruent within ourselves when we are true and honest; when we don't do things against our values that we might feel sorry for later. People are healthiest when they are being congruent. Work settings are healthy and are fostering a true culture of recognition when there is an atmosphere of openness and trust. I suggest we all consider adopting Satir's Five Freedom's as a way of being in our business and organizational environments:

1. The Freedom to see and hear what is here, *instead of what should be, was and/or will be.*

2. The Freedom to say what one feels or thinks *instead of what one "should " say.*

3. The Freedom to feel what one feels *instead of what one "ought" to feel.*

4. The Freedom to ask for what one wants *instead of waiting for permission.*

5. The Freedom to take risks in one's behalf *instead of waiting only to be secure.*

IMPLEMENTING CHANGE

The key element of good change implementation lies in two areas: the first is giving information—and lots of it; and the second is having people buy into the necessity of the change. The change implementation process requires planning for change, preparing new resources and acknowledging and celebrating the process.

There are several steps that must be considered when going through any change:

1. Begin by describing the change as clearly as possible. Visualize what will be different and write and speak of this change as if it had been already implemented.

2. Acknowledge the things you can control and the things you can't. Decide what you can influence if you cannot control a situation. Ask yourself:

   • What strengths can I or my group bring to this process?
   • What obstacles will I have to overcome to create my vision?

3. Describe in detail how you will handle each of the following:

   • Communication:
     —What are you going to add to your existing structure of communication?
     —How will you control the grapevine?
   • Involvement of resources:
     —How will you do it?
     —Who should be included?
     —What should your role be?
     —How will you overcome resistance?
   • Leadership:
     —Who will lead the change?
     —Who will you follow?
     —Who are the people or organizations that will champion the cause?

- Timetable:
  —When will each of the above actions occur?

4. Find out what people and materials are needed. Ask:

   - What new resources will be necessary to achieve this change?
   - Who are the people you can turn to for help?
   - What new skills are required?
   - Is there training available? Do you need to create some?
   - What knowledge must you get hold of?
   - What attitudes must you change? What ones must you adopt?

5. Plan in the recognition. Ask:

   - What incentives can you create to move people along this change?
   - What can you do to motivate yourself?

6. Is there a ritual that you can do to let go of the past?

   - How will you acknowledge and celebrate this change?
   - How will you reward yourself for changing?
   - What does each person involved want to be recognized for?

3

RECOGNITION: THE QUALITY WAY

By now it should be clear that *Recognition: The Quality Way* is an all encompassing attitude of mind. It requires a change in paradigm from the traditional sense of recognition that stops short at reward and incentive plans. Recognition is a way of being with people. It begins with a reminder of the stuff we learned as children—simple acts of courtesy such as a smile and a thank you. To be a true recognition specialist you must be somewhat of a psychologist who understands the principles of motivation as well as the principles for being an effective change agent. From that perspective, you have the opportunity of then being a healer who transforms past hurts by present remembrances. And then it is a short step to allowing people to experience their uniqueness and the full expression of their talents and abilities. That's what people *really* need, not money, fame, or power. *Recognition: The Quality Way* is nothing short of full awareness, appreciation, acknowledgment, and acceptance of human beings as physical, social, psychological, and spiritual beings.

In a survey taken by one of my motivation and productivity classes on why people leave their job, it was found that 75% of the 100 people surveyed had left or considered leaving their current position because of the "lack of growth and recognition on the job." I told that to a friend of mine who is an executive in the coffee export industry in Costa Rica. A week later, he came back and reported to me that the productivity in his office had doubled that week because of what I had said. It seems that this man had been going into work about an hour earlier than everyone else. By the time his staff arrived, he was steeped neck high in contracts and phone calls. He used to greet them as they walked in the door with, "Can you find me that XYZ contract?" or "What did you do with the phone number or rates on QRS?" Not even a good-morning, or a smile to ask how their day was going. He was bypassing the normal niceties of civilization. He told me that during our conversation, he had vowed to himself to make a simple change. When each member of the staff arrived, he stopped long enough to have some small talk and to simply let them know that he was aware of their existence. That one act took about 15–20 minutes of his workday, but added hours to each of theirs! Within a week, the productivity in their work almost doubled.

The simple act of another human being letting us know that they are aware of our existence can radically change the way we feel about ourselves and consequently the way we perform. All of us need to have our self-esteem built because life's "negative imprints" have a way of leaving their mark on us. Henry Ford once said, "Whether you think you can, or think you can't, you are right!" Where do we get the messages that we tell ourselves about whether we can or can't? Usually, they originate outside ourselves. We know that the unconscious mind is an endless recorder and remembers everything that has ever happened or been said to us. We may not consciously remember messages given to us as children, however, they have become "imprinted" and influence our later behavior. Although these imprints can be positive or negative, some believe that more than 75% have been negative. When we are told we are lazy, stupid, or bad as children (and who wasn't, at some point at least), somehow our unconscious minds store these as thoughts that we later play out in unwanted adult behavior. Our negative thoughts later emerge as reality for us. It's a cycle that seems to be message, thought, behavior. Our internal motivation is based first of all on some external stimuli or message. The only way to break the negative message cycle is to hear multiple positive messages. We need to hear positive things spoken to us, or we'll have a hard time conjuring up positive regard for ourselves. Some say we need at least four positive messages to replace every one negative.

We have also been accultured to have a need to please the person in charge. We are conditioned to "grow up" for our parents, to "learn" for our teacher, and to "win" for our coach. We all crave appreciation, and we seem to want that appreciation most from our leader. We might turn that idea around to realize that the key role of a leader then, is the ability to show appreciation. For many managers, the idea of thanking someone for doing the job they were supposed to do is too crazy an idea, but a leader that can support his follower's need for appreciation will have a loyal team, willing to "win one for the Gipper!"

So, although we may not be working to be praised, whether we are willing to admit it or not, we all need praise to keep working or we will continue to be influenced by unconscious negative imprints. In fact, research done on motivation at Harvard University says we CRAVE it. "The deepest principle in human nature is the craving to be appreciated," says Dr. Paul Tournier, M.D. He also said that, "No one can develop freely in this world and find a full life without feeling understood by at least one person . . ." We are not islands unto ourselves. To promote the climate of trust, self-worth, and positive reinforcement needed for a quality environment, spending a great deal of money on elaborate parties and trips—nice as they are—won't help people feel good about themselves if they are filled with negative internal dialogues from the past. The way to change that is simple but not easy. The first step is not an elaborate plan or a committee or a banquet. The first step is to remind ourselves on a daily basis of some of the simple courtesies that perhaps we have forgotten. And then to notice the things we are saying, as well as the things we aren't.

I recently listened to a lecture that underlined this point rather poignantly. The speaker was Barbara Marx Hubbard, author, scholar, and futurist, who was one of the first women to be placed in nomination for the vice-presidency of the United States. In outlining the need for co-creation, she highlighted the concept of the giftedness of each individual and made an interesting analogy that I think is appropriate here. She spoke of our gifts being like mother's milk. When a child does not drink the milk the mother has provided, it actually causes great pain for the mother. When our innate gifts and talents go *unexpressed,* we become shut down! Many studies today show that depression is often caused because creative expression is being stifled in some area of our lives. Just as the child grows and is strengthened by drinking the milk, we actually become more of who we are when someone else acknowledges and receives our gifts. In fact, she goes so far as to suggest that we never actually become fully who we are until who we are has been received and acknowledged by another! Recognition is not something nice to do for someone, it is absolutely necessary for each of us to experience our wholeness. We know who we truly are only in relationship to another who receives us. Recognition of another is an obligation and a privilege we each have towards the progress of human potential. It's a grand concept and of course, we may be tempted to start "programs" to make it happen. I suggest that it is best to start in simple ways.

COMPLIMENTS

We have the opportunity to change lives daily by the words we say, or don't say, to one another. Sometimes we get so caught up in doing "great things" that we forget to do the little things that truly make us great. Many years ago, I decided to make a habit of stopping men on elevators or in other such casual circumstances and making positive comments about their appearance (when appropriate, of course). I've come to become quite a connoisseur of men's ties! It is amazing how many of them smile kind of sheepishly and then tell me that no one else has ever said anything to them about it before. Gender studies are beginning to reveal that compliments from women to men are the rarest, but in general, we are all so quick to correct and so slow to compliment. The simple compliment is one of the gifts we can give in any economy and it's worth is beyond measure. We all feel good when we hear such a positive evaluation that we believe we have earned whether it be of our character, our appearance, or our performance. Later, we'll have a look at what different personalities tend to want to be appreciated for. For now, suffice it to say, complimenting is an art worth learning—and one that needs to be learned.

John D. Rockefeller knew this truth. He believed that understanding these social needs were so important that he frequently said that the ability he'd pay most for was the ability to deal with people. Andrew Carnegie agreed. He once said that you could take away all of his factories and all of his equipment, but leave him his people and he could rebuild the business in less than three years. He understood that people were the most important asset. He hired people like Charles Schwab, to whom he paid over a million dollars a year because he knew "much about people." Schwab described his own success by saying, "I consider my ability to arouse enthusiasm among people the greatest asset I possess, and the way to develop the best that is in a person is by appreciation and encouragement. There is nothing else that so kills the ambitions of a person as criticism from his superiors. I believe in giving a person incentive to work. So I am anxious to praise but loath to find fault. If I like anything, I am hearty in my approbation and lavish in my praise."

Unfortunately, many of us have a tendency to speak when we find fault and remain silent when we find something to praise. We need to reverse this attitude. When was the last time you thanked someone for doing a good job, for working cooperatively, or for working safely? When was the last time you reprimanded someone for being late or for being uncooperative? In the spirit of management by walking around, why not spend at least 15 minutes a day *looking* for positive things to praise? When we open our eyes to find something, we always do.

Perhaps you could institute company brag sessions where each department could have a representative talk about all the "little" things they did each month that have cut costs for the company. One energy company in Texas did this for a while and yielded over $18 million in savings over a two-year period.

LEARNING TO PRAISE

Learning to praise is an art and needs a great deal of practice. Saying thank you is a special form of that art. When someone does something that we want to compliment or are grateful for, many of us give a common passing "good job, I appreciate it" remark. A simple thank you can become profound recognition by following a three-fold method of giving thanks:

- Step one: Make the general remark that you are used to making. Such as, "That was a very good presentation you made, Rob."

- Step two: Tell the person specifically what you liked, what behavior you are especially trying to reinforce. As in, "I particularly liked the way you used humor to make a point about the changes we'll have to make in the department."

- Step three: Generalize from this specific instance to a personality trait or character strength. Such as, "Your sense of humor always gets us through rough times. I sure admire that."

In *I Saw What You Did & I Know Who You Are* (Performance Management, 1990), Janis Allen, a consultant from Atlanta, Georgia, calls using a positive statement about a specific performance a "lead-in to universal praise." "Think of it this way," she says, "If you can name a specific behavior that someone does or has done, and go on to say, 'This conveys your professionalism, your diligence, your eye for detail,' then you've done a good job of reinforcing. You are telling that person, 'This specific event is indicative of something I'm proud of about your habits and I like the way you run your life.' Who couldn't use hearing a remark like that once in a while?"

A smile or a compliment can go a long way. These simple acts are the foundations and part of the first phase of *Recognition: The Quality Way*.

FOUR PHASES

Phase-one recognition is awareness. Awareness implies two things:

- Letting someone know that you know that they exist—that who they are makes a difference; that they matter; that they are important. You can give for free what someone else wants most in life!

- A company culture and atmosphere where people laugh, support each other, and listen to one another on a regular basis. An organization can be said to have a true quality culture when recognition of employees is not something you do once in a quarter, or a year, but is part of the make-up of who you are— an organization that is aware that it's members are its most valuable asset.

Phase-two recognition is appreciation—when we let people know we are grateful for what they have done, both their ordinary job and the things they do above and beyond. If we use the three-fold approach of expressing gratitude, highlighting specific behavior, and then generalizing to a universal quality of the person, we have gone a long way in helping to change those negative imprints. People must first believe in their own quality before they can produce quality work.

Phase-three recognition is acknowledgment. When our compliments and thank you's are universalized to a person's qualities or character, we've begun to understand acknowledgment. Actually, the acknowledgment phase is essential for recognition to have any lasting effect. Becoming master acknowledgers requires understanding human nature, human behavior, and what motivates people. We feel acknowledged when we can say, "they really know me; they really understand who I am." Someone else knows what is important to me, what my real abilities are, what I am most proud of, what my dreams are and what concerns really get my attention. Then, and only then can you say you know what I am. Then I feel acknowledged.

Phase-four recognition is acceptance. When acknowledgment goes a step further, and we really let people know that they are worthwhile individuals, we have moved into the phase of recognition known as acceptance. It is at this phase that recognition progresses from being something nice to do, to a life-changing appreciation of the uniqueness of each individual. When we are accepted, no one has to watch over our shoulder to see that we are working, and we don't have to punch time clocks or explain every coffee break, doctor's appointment, or even a wandering look.

We all need to feel important. We all want to know that someone knows we exist. We want to contribute and be productive. Even Freud acknowledged work as one of the two major human needs! We need to know that our ideas can make a difference. We sometimes need to be reinforced. Above all else, we long to be heard and understood and finally to be accepted for the unique people that we are.

Organizations that know this and are excellent at recognizing people go far in quality improvement efforts. Recognition reinforces desired behaviors and builds empowered employees. A culture of recognition sets up the environment for quality to take place. It is the missing piece in much of the quality literature today. People are more than machines. Some of the ways we address quality seem to forget that. It is imperative that we move beyond the surface of how to DO quality and learn how to BE it.

In the next chapter, I'll summarize what the quality experts (and others) have to say about how to create a quality organization. They all at least mention recognition. We will also look at what their methods imply.

The total quality movement has the opportunity to be the harbinger of a new era in American business. The only way to change is to revolutionize the way we look at ourselves as profit-centered rather than people oriented. Profits are made by people. The organizations that will succeed in the future will be the ones who not only put the customer first, but also every employee and vendor as well. When you develop a culture that puts recognition first, quality follows naturally.

4

WHAT THE EXPERTS SAY
(OR DON'T SAY)
ABOUT RECOGNITION

Whether total quality remains just a buzzword of the 1980s and 1990s depends upon whether or not organizations and corporations simply inaugurate quality programs or truly make a serious culture change. Those who have already begun to make history as quality experts have advocated nothing short of a radical change in the way we do business and the way we perceive management and leadership in our organizations. They also question why we exist and the way we operate—as isolated individuals or organizations who compete rather than as parts of systems that cooperate.

It is rather ironic that among the elite of those who advocate quality, while there has been a great deal of mutual respect, there has been very little attempt at cooperation—and so even those on the quality bandwagon are following "Deming's 14 points" or "Juran's trilogy" or are carrying the Crosby banner. Some of the lesser-known quality consultants have begun to devise their own nomenclature and "must do's" and create yet a greater divergence in the very concept that was meant to unite.

It is beyond the scope of this book to attempt to analyze or synthesize what's been said or what's being done on all different fronts. But, at the risk of being over-simplistic, this chapter attempts to summarize what each of the "loudest voices" to date have had to say about what it means to be dedicated to quality. Because this is a book on recognition, the prime focus of this chapter will be to cite direct quotes where available, and to look at the implications of what each of the main teachings have to say about recognition as part of the overall quality movement.

A search of the literature shows that although the quality experts mention recognition somewhere within their exposés of their individual theses, no one gives very much attention to what recognition really means or how, in practice, it is to be carried out. Recognition still gets mixed up with bonuses, incentives, and rewards. Many of my ideas and much of this book comes from what I have personally read into, extrapolated, or inferred from each of the works, and in some instances, the way companies who are using the particular brand of quality have interpreted the writings and works of the quality experts. I expect to bring the consciousness of the need for quality recognition to a new level, which has up to now, in most instances, merely been implied rather than truly practiced—somewhat like the quality movement itself.

It is my hope that the person who is new to the quality movement will find this chapter to be an enlightening overview, and the seasoned quality person will find it a succinct summary and a cause for further reflection.

HISTORY

The concept of quality has been around long before the term total quality management or continuous process improvement became popular. Many of the tools and processes that are currently touted under the quality umbrella have been in existence for more than half a century and the Chinese have records that show a focus on quality more than 2,000 years ago.

Some consider Walter Shewhart to be the grandfather of the modern quality movement as such. In 1924, while working for Bell Labs, he developed a set of statistical charts for the control of product variables. In 1931, in his book *Economic Control of Quality of Manufactured Product,* he explained the necessity of finding and eliminating local sources of trouble in a process and allowing it to remain in statistical control. All of this must occur before innovations leading to improved productivity can be achieved. Shewhart might have remained a relative unknown had his cause not been taken up and applied by W.E. Deming.

While working for the Bureau of the Census in early 1941, Deming had already showed that the introduction of quality control in clerical operations saved the bureau several thousand dollars. But Americans were not yet ready for Deming or for the concepts of statistical quality control.

After World War II, American companies were the primary producers for the world. In 1946, the American Society for Quality Control was formed. However, there was a complacent attitude toward quality at that time because the US was in a post-war boom and was fast becoming a production-driven, high-consumption environment.

Deming had spent time in Japan in 1946 and 1948 to work on the census as well as agricultural and other demographic studies. While there, he developed acquaintances among Japanese statisticians. He began to tell them how important they were and what they could do for their economy.

In 1950, Deming was invited by JUSE, the Union of Japanese Scientists and Engineers, to teach about statistical methods in industry. At that time, 45 managers agreed to attend seminars and to commit to a top-down approach to quality in their organizations. Quality in Japan, in addition to being a result of techniques, began to become management policy!

Meanwhile, in America, during the late 1940s, Joseph Juran began to develop what may have been the most influential course on the subject of quality management. He offered "Managing for Quality" for almost 30 years through the American Management Association. Early on, he saw the broadening role of quality, and urged quality professionals to prepare for it.

Juran, a popular free-lance advisor and implementer of quality management methods, was invited to Japan in 1954. He specialized in teaching managers how to find and eliminate the causes of poor quality. It has been said that Dr. Juran's visit marked a transition in Japan's quality control activities from dealing primarily with technology that was based in manufacturing factories, to an overall concern for the entire management. For that he received the Order of the Sacred Treasure.

By the 1960s, Juran had begun to report to Americans on the new ideas on quality coming out of Japan. But, the turning point in the US didn't really occur until the early 1970s, when Japanese products began to invade American markets, especially in the automotive and consumer electronics industries. American management had still not yet realized that the Japanese were able to produce—and therefore sell—at lower costs because of their excellent quality management techniques.

To this day, the Juran Institute continues to be one of the major leaders in the field, focusing on the cost of quality, planning and management issues, and employee motivation. It continues to focus on teaching managers to take charge of their quality programs.

Philip Crosby became a popular quality control specialist and his now famous books, *Quality is Free* (New American Library, 1979) and *Quality Without Tears* (McGraw-Hill, 1984), also describe explicit techniques for teaching quality control methods to management. Crosby was vice-president and director for corporate quality for ITT in 1968 when he gave his famous "elevator speech" to the conglomerate's CEO Harold S. Geneen on route to the 13th floor of their building. He cited that 20% of the corporate annual sales went into the cost of not doing something right. In 1979, he was instrumental in aiding the Tennant Corporation, a maintenance machine company, to lower their defect rates by 52%, thereby reducing the cost of errors to 8.9% of sales, down from 17%. Crosby was quoted in *Business Week* as claiming that "the US worker is among the most able in the world, and that 80% of defects result purely from management decisions."

The beginning of the quality movement is often traced to June 24, 1980, when NBC broadcasted a documentary entitled, "If Japan Can . . . Why Can't We?" Because world competition had been steadily increasing, American managers began to be less complacent and were now willing to look for new ways to improve productivity. Customers were voting with their feet and buying non-American products because they were of better quality. Executives began sending people to Japan to find out how to achieve quality. At first, we imported the concept of quality circles, which involved letting groups of workers meet to suggest improvement. Few American managers were trained to properly direct this effort, and so it failed miserably. The quality movement learned from this to focus more on leadership and understanding people as well as on measurement.

Many of the components of the quality movement as we know it today are taken from the Japanese model.

What we still need to learn from the Japanese is how to eliminate competition and work through cooperation. In America, most of our companies still focus on how to beat the competition rather than on how to offer better service to the public and employees. But, we are learning. At least we are beginning to try to understand what quality truly is about.

DEFINITION

Total quality is a concept that seems to elude precise definition. Over time and in different circumstances, it has come to mean a variety of things. Some say that quality is about meeting product specification. The American Society for Quality Control (ASQC) and the American National Standards Institute suggest that it is "the totality of features and characteristics of a product or service that bear on its ability to satisfy a given need." Crosby defines it as "conformance to requirements" and Juran says it is "fitness for use." A quality product is one that is "free from deficiencies" for the user and the producer. Quality can be gauged by the cost to make it right, without excessive rework and the accompanying waste involved.

Others insist that quality is a comprehensive vision of continuous improvement shared by all members of an organization. Tom Peters, for example, would adhere to the Webster's definition as "a degree of excellence."

Still others define quality in terms of the consumer. They see it as "meeting and exceeding customer expectations," which they believe breeds customer loyalty and ultimately product and company success. According to Dr. Armand V. Feigenbaum, it is "the total composite product and service characteristics of marketing, engineering, manufacturing, and maintenance through which the product and service in use will meet the expectations of the customer." Quality isn't what advertisers or engineers say it is. It's what the buyer says it is.

If you talk to a number of different consultants or quality managers (who have a variety of titles), you will come away confused at best. How can we sort out this confusion? What most organizations are defining as their quality process is an amalgam of ideas from one or several of the "quality experts." One of the most pragmatic definitions of total quality management that I have seen to date comes from Dan Stowell and Lucinda Hunt, quality consultants from Southbury, CT who combine what is best from each of the others to say:

> "Total quality management is the application of concepts, tools, and processes through management, leadership, and employee involvement to achieve complete customer satisfaction and continuous improvement in every area of the organization."

What follows is an attempt to summarize the basic tenets of each of these leaders, not meant to be the definitive analysis, but simply a jumping off point to discuss the role of recognition in this movement. I have attempted to report their opinions (not necessarily mine). I will introduce each of the people who have had a major influence, describing both their overall philosophy and in most cases, the methods that a company must follow to adhere to that philosophy.

QUALITY EXPERTS AND PIONEERS

Ishikawa

Kaoru Ishikawa, one of Japan's most noted quality control practitioners, was a student under both Deming and Juran in the 1950s. He has written several books on the subject of industrial quality control, including *Guide to Quality Control* (Quality Resources, 1986); which is used throughout the world as a guide to collecting and interpreting data for determining product defects.

Key Concepts:

- Worker participation.

- Quality teams and circles—designed to work in natural work groupings because those doing the work know where the problems are and must be seen as the key in implementing solutions (replaced by cross-functional work teams).

- Training in rudimentary techniques to generate ideas and to investigate problems—instructional methods that can reach even an unsophisticated audience with some sophisticated ideas.

- Statistics rarely used. (We will see that this is a great contrast to some of the other quality approaches.)

- Supervisors who have effective interpersonal management skills.

- Participative team management approach.

- Group mission in alignment with the corporate mission.

Although quality circles are no longer popular, the concept of "empowerment" still is. Employees are given both the authority to make decisions and the tools necessary to do so. This includes training in systematic problem solving and in working together effectively in a group. Ishikawa has questioned whether Americans can readily implement some of these quality methods because of the difference in societal structures, pay systems, the lifetime employment system in Japan, religion, and the way the Japanese develop relationships with subcontractors. He especially emphasizes the fact that American managers use a system of management that punishes employees for quality problems and gives no decision-making powers to workers. Practicing true quality control, according to Ishikawa, is ". . . to develop, design, produce, and supply a quality product and service that is most economical, most useful, and always satisfactory to the consumer." He suggests that this continuous process takes as many as 10 years to develop and it cannot be developed by quality control specialists. It requires nothing short of an overhaul in top-down attitudes towards managing people.

What we can infer from Ishakawa's legacy to quality is that organized mechanisms for ensuring that enough recognition is given must be in place from the start. Many organizations depend on recognition being more spontaneous, just as previously they had depended upon problem solving and group participation being natural. And we know from experience that that just doesn't happen.

Unfortunately, most quality circles that have received awards have received them because of savings made for the corporation. This has the effect of having teams feel that the only valued contributions are those that generate tangible benefits. The real feeling of group ownership can begin to be undermined because they begin to realize that certain "problems" are more important to solve and may fail to look at new problems that haven't already been given management approval. This defeats the whole point of group initiative in finding the appropriate problems in the first place.

The key here is that the process must be rewarded as well as the result, and is in fact, even more important. What must be recognized is a group's ability to use an organized problem-solving structure as well as its enthusiasm and commitment. The question that arises is, how can this be measured?

Mike Robson, an acknowledged international authority on quality circles, set out to recommend criteria for team/circle recognition in what he called the *Journey to Excellence* (John Wiley, 1986):

- **Effort and attitude** (weight approximately 30%):

    — Membership (participation, self-development, and improved problem-solving ability).
    — Operations (leadership, cooperation, and training).
    — Meetings (preparation, scheduling, and documentation).
    — Follow-up (complete assignment and tracking in place).

- **Technique and procedure** (weight approximately 30%):

    — Objective selection (relevant to team/circle, relevant to organization, and clearly understood and documented).
    — Action plans (practical, well understood, and well implemented).
    — Discussion/investigation (problems well understood, date complete and correct, proper evaluation, and thorough discussion by team/circle).
    — Checking (consistency with accepted practices and tracking appropriate).
    — Reports (well organized and complete, on time, and well presented).

- **Accomplishment of objective** (weight approximately 30%):

    — Problem solved (base cause identified and corrected and reoccurrence prevented).

— Analysis complete (data evaluated and measures and tracking evaluated).

— Solution optimum/practical (best potential solution chosen, and implementation achievable and reasonable).

— Implementation effective (directly attacks problem, and shows improvement in reasonable time/effort).

— Follow-up measurement (tracking system in place, and periodic review in place).

• **Value of accomplishment** (weight approximately 10%)

— Value assessment (direct elimination of inefficient use of time, resources, and dollars).

Bonus weighting of 10% should be considered where solution demonstrates exceptional originality or inventiveness.

Tom Peters

Tom Peters, though not directly considered a Quality expert, is definitely an advocate of participative corporate cultures and so I believe deserves mention when fostering a recognition culture.

Key Concepts

• A single strategic focus.

• A penchant for excellence.

• An understanding of company mission and values.

• A stress on the importance of customer values.

• A systems view of the company—comprised of all people who are effected by the company, its products, or services—and these include the vendors or suppliers, the workers, managers, shareholders, and customers.

- Strong emphasis on interpersonal fellowship and a keen sense of interdependence among all stakeholders.

To accomplish this, these authors suggest using corporate models that have achieved a reputation for quality. This is perhaps the greatest strength and weakness in this method. Models, who are truly following a process of continuous improvement, are moving targets, at best, and may not always stay on top. While emulating them, you may find that they no longer deserve the emulation! Many of the companies, for example, that Peters once called "excellent" have disappeared, or at least have fallen from grace.

Much of the emphasis on creating excellence is focused at the executive level in an organization. If it isn't happening from the top, it can't happen. So, most of what they feel it takes to be successful in a quality effort depends on the skills of the leaders. In fact, it depends entirely on true leadership rather than management in the traditional sense.

For these authors, true leaders have the skills to activate the direction they have set. They are able to link the strategic direction to the practical activities of the various groups within the organization. They are able to make the theoretical practical and turn ideas into actions.

The role of management, then, is to develop and maintain the systems that are then set up to track whatever would be the leader's stated valued dimensions. Tracking would therefore include statistical process control (SPC) and quality engineering methods. The rest of the organization must then develop the skills for individual control in responding to executive leadership. The system becomes a circle with each piece integrally connected. People, and the consequent recognition of these people, are essential in such a system.

Tom Peters, however, states that most organizations take a negative view of their people. "Companies verbally berate participants for poor performance; they call for risk taking but punish even tiny failures; they want innovation, but kill the spirit of the champion; with their rationalist hats on, they design systems that seem calculated to tear down their worker's self-image."

In his search for companies that reflected "excellence," Peters noted some common threads laced throughout the findings. All of these excellent companies designed systems to reinforce the notion that most of their people were winners. They believed in the people they hired. There was a rich culture surrounding the companies that provided the dominant use of anecdotes, myths, and legends that conveyed the organization's shared values. In addition, these excellent companies had a strong sense of respect for the individual. They gave people control over their destinies; they helped make meaning for people. Peters noted that although most top managers asserted that their companies cared for their people, the excellent companies were distinguished by the intensity and persuasiveness of this concern—in other words, their ability to keep recognition at the heart of their corporate culture.

Peters drives home the point that the most commonly practiced crime in industry today is a fundamental insensitivity toward personal dignity. "Criticism should not include contempt, because it is the accumulation of little slights that kills the spirit (and with it the possibility of excellent performance). *Respect* is the key. Respect for all people. Respect is caring and trust. Respect is presence." This is the heart of the philosophy he advocates.

"Management must be wandering, listening, staying in touch, and caring enough to build a relationship with the staff—it's like a magic potion. It works. It gives management the opportunity to see with their own eyes and hear with their own ears "the reality of life" for the staff and the working environment."

Armand Feigenbaum

Feigenbaum developed a philosophy of *Total Quality Control* (McGraw-Hill, 1990)—one of the premier texts on quality improvement. Feigenbaum, an MIT engineer, is president and chief executive of General Systems Co., in Pittsfield, MA. He stresses that all of the approaches to quality have to be synergistic. You get no quality improvement from a system that is not dedicated to quality in every aspect of its operation.

Key Concepts

- Executive leadership with a passion around quality issues.

- Long-term sustained commitment—not a one time, quick-fix solution.

- Using effective instructional methods to create an integrating theme, which can have organization-wide implementation.

- Quality as a technology that can be systemized and taught.

- Managers who have masterful interpersonal management skills in handling change and creative innovation.

- Hands-on implementation.

- Team leadership.

Feigenbaum stresses that each individual contributes skills to a diverse work force and must have access to resources and accurate information to be effective. The way to recognize employees is to be certain that they have all that they need to get a job done effectively and to be certain that employees skills are acknowledged and put to good use. Diversity, rather than conformity, is to be encouraged and applauded.

Philip Crosby

Crosby places his emphasis on effective quality management. His philosophy can be summed up by acknowledging that it's cheaper to produce higher quality. "Do things right in the first place, and you won't have to pay to fix them or do them over." If you track the cost of quality, you will be guided to areas where you can make the greatest improvement in both quality and efficiency.

Key Concepts

- Emphasis on cost of quality as the only performance measurement.

- Zero defects as the only performance standard.

- Methods that include a continual quality audit.

He advocates a 14-step approach to implementing quality in an organization:

1. *Insure management commitment.* There must be agreement that quality improvement is the only practical way to profit improvement. He underlines the difference between long-term communication and short-term motivation. Quality improvement takes patience and time.

2. *Form quality improvement teams (QITs).* Teams are formed by gathering representatives of each department who have the power to commit the department to action. (Note that this is different from the cross-functional teams that others advocate.)

3. *Use measurement to determine where current and potential quality problems lie.* All work must be subject to measurement, and he insists that all departments find where their work is subject to error and visibly chart their progress.

4. *Evaluate the cost of quality.* This must be done by the comptroller's office and is an indication of where correcting defects will result in greater company profit.

5. *Raise quality awareness and personal concern of all members.* This is done by alerting employees to the cost of non-quality. ALL employees must be educated to understand and appreciate this process and managers and supervisors must be trained to communicate this awareness.

6. *Take actions to correct problems.* Meetings need to be held within each department so that those actually doing the work can discover and disclose the problem areas so that they can immediately be addressed wherever appropriate.

7. *Establish committee for zero defects program.* Each company must select a small group of people who can uniquely teach the concept of zero defects in that organization.

8. *Train supervisors.* This must be done in a formal way before implementing any of the steps of the process. Managers must not only understand the concepts, but also be able to explain it to their people.

9. *Hold a "zero defects day."* This should be held for all employees on the same day and its purpose is to launch the "new attitude" for long-lasting effects.

10. *Set goals.* Goals are set by employees together with supervisors and must be specific and measurable. Tasks should be assigned 30-, 60-, or 90-day priority.

11. *Encourage employees to communicate obstacles to management.* This is to be done on a simple one-page form so that the appropriate group can develop a solution. All problems must be addressed within 24 hours.

12. *Recognition.* People are to be awarded for meeting their goals or for doing something outstanding. The recognition should not be tied to the obstacles communicated in the last step, because that is not to be seen as a suggestion system but as a real opportunity for employee input on error-cause removal.

Crosby makes it clear that prizes or awards should not be financial because recognition itself is what is important. He underlines that "genuine recognition of performance is something people really appreciate." He even goes so far as to say, "They will continue to support the program, whether or not they, as individuals, participate in the awards. People really don't work for money. They go to work for it, but once the salary has been established, their concern is appreciation. Recognize their contribution publicly and noisily, but don't demean them by applying a price tag to everything."

"Recognition must be given for achieving specific goals worked out in advance, and the employees must have the opportunity to help select the goals. The contest and the measurement are the key. The prize is not significant. It only matters that all of an individual's contemporaries know that he or she has fought the good fight and won.

Above all, individuals must know that management seriously needs their help and sincerely appreciates it."

13. *Establish quality councils.* The in-house quality professionals need to gather with the team chairpeople regularly to be certain the the program is moving smoothly.

14. *Do it all over again.* Crosby's program takes about a year to eighteen months but when it is complete, the cycle simply begins again. It is never over. The process just keeps repeating.

To follow this type of program, team leadership skills, group problem-solving skills, and problem-solving techniques must be developed for an organization to be effective. SPC and quality assurance engineering are essential tools for measuring progress. There must be interdepartmental collaboration as well as the encouragement of individual contribution of skills. Crosby advocates white-collar approaches and management skills that draw out participation. Total participation and commitment to zero defects is the key.

Joseph Juran

Quality, for Juran, is "fitness for use." In American business, quality translates as fitness for sale. Therefore, those who market, design, manufacture, and service the product must know the customer.

Key Concepts

- Design of products that are high-quality and manufacturable to consistent high-quality standards.

- Engineering applications.

- Task teams through whom problems and opportunities need to be identified and solved.

His is a 10-step plan:

1. Build awareness of the need and opportunity for improvement.

2. Set goals for improvement.

3. Organize to reach the goals (establish a quality council, identify problems, select projects, appoint teams, and designate facilitators).

4. Provide training.

5. Carry out projects to solve problems.

6. Report progress.

7. Give recognition.

For Juran, recognition is "public acknowledgment of the successes that are related to quality improvement. Success consists primarily of results traceable to completed improvement projects. Auxiliary successes consist of such things as taking training courses and submitting nominations for projects." In *Leadership for Quality* (The Free Press, 1989), Juran lists the types of recognition he suggests:

- Certificates, plaques, and the like, awarded for serving as a facilitator, completing training courses, or serving on project teams.

- Project teams present their final report in the office of the ranking local manager.

- Project summaries are published in the company news media, along with team pictures. Many companies have created special news supplements or special newsletters devoted to quality improvements.

- Dinners are held to honor project teams.

- Prizes are awarded to teams judged to have completed the "best" projects during some designated time period.

Published accounts of successful projects serve not only to provide recognition; they also serve as case materials for training purposes, and as powerful stimulators to all.

He distinguishes recognition from "rewards" defining rewards as salary increases, bonuses, and promotions keyed to job performance and usually conferred in private. Recognition primarily consists of "ceremonial" actions (typically nonfinancial in nature) taken to publicize meritorious performance. These usually focus on improvements, while rewards focus on conduct of operations using performance appraisal or merit rating.

Juran encourages senior managers to preside at ceremonial awards of certificates or plaques to persons who have completed training and to participate in dinner meetings specifically organized to honor teams that have completed their quality-improvement projects. Often the awards are publicized through such vehicles as a company newsletter or bulletin board and occasionally through the local press. Similar meetings are organized to recognize outstanding contributions made by suppliers.

It is the reward system (e.g., merit ratings and bonuses) that best indicates to employees what managers really consider to be priorities. "The reward system not only serves its basic purpose of rewarding human performance; it also serves to inform all concerned of the senior managers' priorities. If the goals are revised (to total quality), but the reward system is not, the result as viewed by subordinates is conflicting signals. Most subordinates resolve this conflict by following the priorities of the reward system."

Managers must also beware that what they perceive as rewards are really serving as rewards instead of punishments. "Financial incentives are deceptively attractive. They look good while pay is going up—during that part of the cycle they are 'bonuses' for good work. It all changes when the work turns poor and the removal of bonuses results in lower pay. Now, it is no longer an incentive system; it has become a system of 'penalties' with all the accompanying argument about who is responsible. Nonfinancial incentives avoid the pitfall of bonuses becoming penalties, but must be kept above the gimmicky level."

8. Communicate results.

9. Keep score.

10. Maintain momentum by making annual improvement part of the regular system.

To be successful, members of an organization must have knowledge of the user needs and a clear understanding of how the user/customer uses the product or service. There must be a great deal of collaboration or teamwork between engineering, manufacturing, and customer service. Quality cannot be left in the hands of designers and engineers because when it is, the message that is received is that quality is the domain of one department only. "Quality is everyone's responsibility."

W. Edwards Deming

Statistical quality (process) control is a philosophy that places emphasis on process rather than product. In this way, you can be assured of preventing quality slippage rather than spending time fixing after it has slipped. Competitive quality cannot be attained by traditional quality-control inspection methods which emphasized the end product rather than the process of getting to it.

Workers aren't the problem with quality, neither are managers—it's the systems that management has installed that produce bad quality. Therefore, for quality management to work, the systems must be changed—by senior management. Management, according to Deming, must become "profoundly knowledgeable" about people, processes, and the interactions between them. There are four parts to a system of profound knowledge: appreciation for a system, knowledge about variation, theory of knowledge, and an understanding of psychology. This is best described in his last book, *The New Economics,* published in 1993 by MIT's Center for Advanced Engineering Study.

Two of the highlights of Deming's four-day quality seminars were the red-bead experiment and the funnel experiment. The red-bead experiment sought to prove that improving a product or service is the job of management—who must improve the system that produces the product or service. He used the funnel experiment to illustrate the importance of understanding variation.

The Japanese took the original Shewhart cycle that Deming had taught them and renamed it the Deming cycle. It is basically a four-step process for quality improvement:

1. Plan—to improve a process or product.

2. Do—what is planned.

3. Study—the results.

4. Act—on what has been learned.

The process is then repeated and continuously improved.

Deming believed that for a quality program to work, there must be universal participation—executives and managers must adopt quality control methods into their decision making and model the process. Statistical methods must be emphasized, but he proposed a 14-step plan as a prerequisite to implementing SPC. This plan, was revised and rewritten by Lloyd Dobyns and Clare Crawford-Mason, who worked on the famous NBC documentary, "If Japan Can, Why Can't We?":

1. Create constancy of purpose for the improvement of product and service, with the aim to become competitive, stay in business, and provide jobs.

2. Adopt the new philosophy of cooperation (win-win) in which everybody wins. Put it into practice and teach it to employees, customers, and suppliers.

3. Cease dependency on mass inspection to achieve quality. Improve the process and build quality into the product in the first place.

4. End the practice of awarding business on the basis of price alone. Instead, minimize total cost in the long run. Move toward a single supplier for any one item, on a long-term relationship of loyalty and trust.

5. Improve constantly and forever the system of production, service, planning, or any activity. This will improve quality and productivity and thus constantly decrease costs.

6. Institute training for skills.

7. Adopt and institute leadership for the management of people, recognizing their different abilities, capa-

bilities, and aspirations. The aim of leadership should be to help people, machines, and gadgets do a better job. Leadership of management is in need of overhaul, as well as leadership of production workers.

8. Drive out fear and build trust so that everyone can work effectively.

9. Break down barriers between departments. Abolish competition and build a win-win system of cooperation within the organization. People in research, design, sales, and production must work as a team to foresee problems of production and in use that might be encountered with the product or service.

10. Eliminate slogans, exhortations, and targets asking for zero defects or new levels of productivity. Such exhortations only create adversarial relationships, as the bulk of the causes of low quality and low productivity belong to the system and thus lie beyond the power of the work force.

11. Eliminate numerical goals, numerical quotas, and management by objectives. Substitute leadership.

12. Remove barriers that rob people of joy in their work. This will mean abolishing the annual rating or merit system that ranks people and creates competition and conflict.

13. Institute a vigorous program of education and self-improvement.

14. Put everybody in the company to work to accomplish the transformation. The transformation is everybody's job.

Key Concepts

- Strong executive leadership.

- Modeling of the underlying ethics behind a quality effort.

- Organization-wide participation.

- A commitment to process control, and abandonment of inspection.

- Strong supervisory leadership.

- Training for all, not just the technical, traditional quality professionals.

Specifically regarding recognition, he has been quoted frequently for saying, "Rewards motivate people to work for rewards" (a point that is brought home vehemently by Alfie Kohn in his book, *Punished by Rewards*, Houghton Mifflin Co., 1993). In his seminar, he tells a story that further illustrates this point.

> A man, not an employee of the hotel, picked up my bag at the registration desk of a hotel in Detroit, and carried it to my room. The bag was heavy. I was exhausted and hungry, hoping to get into the dining room before it would close at 11 p.m. I was ever so grateful to him; fished out two dollar bills for him. He refused them. I had hurt his feelings, trying to offer money to him. He had carried the bags for me, not for pay. My attempt to pay him was, in effect, an attempt to change our relationship. I meant well, but did the wrong thing. I resolved to be careful.

One of Deming's primary teachings was that management should create the condition in which people will be treated with dignity and respect, conditions that are their right and in which they thrive, develop, and make their greatest contributions. He believed in a company's need to focus on long-term commitment to its employees and products instead of short-term commitment to financial results. He talked often about people's right to joy in work, which is greatly influenced by their ability to learn and to improve how their work is done. He, himself, was both an example and an advocate of lifelong learning. In *Out of Crisis* (MIT Center for Advanced Engineering Study, 1986) he said, "The possibility of pride of workmanship means more to a production worker than gymnasiums, tennis courts, and recreation areas." And later, "Give the work force a chance to work with pride, and the percent that apparently don't care will erode itself by peer pressure."

Rather than give out rewards, according to Deming, management should create the conditions in which people will be treated with dignity and respect. All people have a right to that, and thrive best and make their best contribution in this atmosphere. Deming sought at all costs to eliminate fear and drive out competition. He hated the "I win-you lose" attitude that seems to be so American. He believed strongly that we can never be satisfied when some people come out ahead at the expense of others. The foundation for innovation and subsequent continuous improvement was a belief in individual dignity. He believed that creativity and a joy in learning are best fostered in a person of high self-esteem. He always showed the deepest appreciation for anyone who could help him to learn and although he was known as an impatient man, he showed the greatest patience when he believed that someone wished to learn. He emphasized that managers and workers as well as all students and children are destroyed by systems which rank, rate, and grade. Instead, he advocated recognizing and honoring differences.

CONCLUSION

Some of the messages we have been receiving about recognition in the quality movement have been contradictory. Unfortunately, in most of the writings of the "quality experts," recognition and rewards have been considered to be synonymous. Behind all of the pie charts and point list-ings, however, is the plea to listen to the person who is closest to the work in order to find out how to improve the work. That's a start. I'd like to take what this implies a step further and say, that when we listen to the person closest to the work, the work improves. There must be a change in focus from the WORK to the PERSON. When we get too busy looking at the end result, we forget our humanness.

5

CELEBRATING DIFFERENCES

Many times, when I am doing team building workshops, managers who believe that they are recognizing their employees well come to discover that they are giving their people what THEY want to receive. This is true for families and friends as well. How often have you received a gift and even been told, "It's exactly what I would have wanted to receive." There is a basic tendency in all of us that wants to treat other people like ourselves. Actually, there's a Judeo-Christian belief that says, "Do unto others as you would have them do unto you." The key word here is "as." Note, it does not say, exactly in the same manner, or in the way you want it. People are different. How they want to receive recognition and what they want to be recognized for, therefore, also differ.

Phase one—awareness—involves some change of attitude, but it is actually relatively easy to do. Even phase two—appreciation—though it may take practice and feel awkward at first, is fairly easily achievable. Phase three—acknowledgment—actually demands that we become students of human nature and learn to be acutely aware of differences. While this study could fill libraries, this chapter gives us a place to begin.

We noted earlier that there are several age/stage theories of motivation. I have come to the conclusion that these age/stage theories do more to help the need of individuals to categorize others. They do not help them understand themselves. So many people feel "abnormal" because they do not have the same time line as their peers. The truth is, there are many factors, in addition to chronological age or lifestage that make us different. *Recognition: The Quality Way* requires that we acknowledge individuals uniquely. So, it would serve us first to know and understand several different approaches to understanding some of those differences.

Instruments to test personality and differences have proliferated during the past few years, and more and more consulting and training companies are establishing new methods to categorize and hopefully, better understand people. What we really need is a computer program that could define a person according to all the different categories—including their personality type, learning style, birth order, metaprograms, brain dominance, hand preference, work style, and favorite ice cream flavors! Given all of that information, I contend that no two profiles would be identical and we would come to a great sense of appreciation for our differences.

Don't get me wrong. I am not *against* instruments. In fact, I use several and will be referring to some below. I am *for* recognizing that differences DO exist and that managers, as well as all human beings, acknowledge this and learn to adapt to the differences in our day to day dealings with other people.

We are all created equal—or are we? All of us are more alike than we are different. But, then it's also true that we are all more different than we are alike. Every encounter could lead us to say, "How alike we are," and at the same time, "How different." Understanding differences is at the heart of learning about the kind of recognition this book is addressing. What we are really concerned with here is not how much alike or different we are, but how we can celebrate and use our differences. The main message in this chapter is that we manage and work with many different kinds of people. If I assume that you are motivated in the same way that I am, I am going to recognize you the way I would want to be recognized. I have felt most recognized (inadvertently) in the past by those who are most like me and who like to receive recognition the same way I do. But, the fact is, everyone is not like me! And so, it's time to make some of the differences more apparent.

First, we need to understand our own styles so we can discern when we are using our own filters to recognize another. As we learn more about who we are, and make the effort to be as authentic as possible, then we can start to notice, respect, appreciate, and even celebrate differences. Learning more about ourselves then, is a noble goal and the best place to begin to be a better manager and motivator.

We need then to answer the questions, "What makes me feel recognized?" and "How do I know when I am appreciated?" When we discover both the type of recognition we need and the ways that we can best receive it, we then can become aware that there are a lot of people who lean towards an opposite approach and that we have to adjust some of our techniques so that we meet *their* needs as well. Self-insight never seems to end. I used to think I was pretty "good" at knowing myself and at recognizing other people's accomplishments. I discover new areas to improve daily. I have come, therefore, to believe that the opposite of *excellence,* is "good." When we are "good" we may never get to be excellent because we're satisfied with where we are. So, I challenge each of us to constantly ask the question, "How can I continuously improve?"

Some people believe that the more discipline there is in a work environment and the more hard work there is, the better people respond. And then there are other people for whom managing an organization means creating an atmosphere of love, humor, and affection. They believe that people only work when they "like" who they are with and what they are doing and are having fun. For others it is a case of pure intellectual stimulation. "Let's get the troops challenged; let's get them thinking." If you do that, you have created a good work environment. Another approach suggests, "Let's help the employees be creative, let them go beyond wherever they are. It is my business to empower others." Where do you fit most of the time? Is that where your staff and co-workers are as well? Recognition depends first on the environment we choose to create. How well do we know our own style?

I often speak at conferences. To get better at my craft, I usually stay and watch the other presenters. Each presenter has a distinct style. Most of us don't pay enough attention to how our style compares to those around us and therefore only meet the needs of a small group of people. If you are beginning to say, "There's no way I can meet everybody's needs," you are probably beginning to hear the message of this book. Life's a game of constant stretching beyond what we thought we could previously do. And so, however adept at adapting to styles you believe you are, work at it just a little bit more. The next time you make a presentation or are having difficulty at work or at home for example, figure out what person you aren't reaching and challenge yourself to change your approach to reach out to meet *that* person's needs.

We'll be discussing several models for understanding differences and practical methods for changing your own approach to meet these differences in a bit. After a while, you'll be able to unconsciously adapt without struggling. For now, begin by looking at differences.

Everybody sees the world differently. We see people differently. We see colors differently. Do you ever wonder if you see the same thing as another person looking at the same object? Does the color green or blue look the same to you as it does to me? This is one of those questions for a philosophy class. It has a modern version in the popular and wonderful story of the five blind men who feel an elephant: Each of them tries to describe what they see and each of them "sees" something different—"It's like a rope; it's like a tree. . . ." What you see depends on your perspective.

We rarely experience things in a definitive way. To quote a principle from the Yogi Master, Amrit Desai: "Don't believe everything you see. Don't believe everything you hear. Don't believe everything you believe!" All beliefs that we have are potentially false. Anything we believe is simply our perception. This belief that some might label "new age" is really very old. It reminds me of Plato's *Allegory of the Cave*, where he talks about the difference between reality and perception. He basically said the same thing, that perception *is* reality. Wayne Dyer in his book, *You'll See It When You Believe It* (Morrow, 1989), made popular the principle that we don't believe what we see anymore, we see what we believe.

Let me give you an example. A friend of mine, who was going through a divorce, told me that his wife was coming to move furniture out the next day. He was very tense, and he said to me, "Tomorrow is going to be a vicious day." And I said, "Well, if you wake up tomorrow morning and decide it is going to be a vicious day, I'll guarantee you are going to have a vicious day. But suppose you wake up tomorrow morning and say, 'This is going to be a good day. I'm going to make this work in spite of the fact that we're negotiating over who gets the house and who gets the coffee table. It's not going to be a fun day, not one of the better days in my life, but it doesn't have to be vicious.' "

He immediately said, "I never thought about it that way." If he had gone into that day feeling it was going to be terrible, he and his wife would have fought all day long. But he now had a new option and knew he could make some changes.

When I spoke to him the next day, of course I asked him what kind of day it was. The quintessential cook, he said "My spice rack is still here!" Then he added, "It wasn't such a bad day after all." That's the amazing power we have: We can control what we see. We can decide what it is we want to see.

That's true about us as managers and motivators as well. What do you see in yourself? What do you want to see? As a trainer, I used to feel that "live" training was the only way. I couldn't believe that training was effective when someone only used computers or videos. I didn't care how good it was. And yet I studied and used some of these things. Why? Because I realized that when I say I don't believe in computer-based training (CBT), it's because I don't learn that way. I really tried to be open to the fact that there are people who do. I couldn't believe it, I couldn't imagine it, and yet there are statistics that show that there are people who learn that way! It was hard for me as the president of a training company not to say that everyone must learn my way. And it would have been very hard to make corporate decisions about this if I weren't highly sensitive to the recognition that there are people who learn that way very effectively.

One of the other more profound life teachings and dilemmas worth pondering is the relationship between unity and duality. So much emphasis in our world is placed on duality. Looking at life through a dual lens, we create competition and separateness. For the purposes of this book, rather than speak of duality, we will look at what appears to be dual as opposite ends of a unified spectrum. The work of the Swiss psychoanalyst Carl Jung has led us to review all of life in terms of polarities. Like the law from physics, every action has an equal and opposite reaction. We all develop physical preferences (e.g., being right or left handed) and we develop psychological preferences as well (e.g., some people see life and notice details, while others observe what is possible or what they believe what they are seeing represents). By understanding these preference opposites, we'll come to an awareness of the diverse ways people need to be recognized as well as our need for each other, and therefore for teams. We can then analyze our current recognition programs and make necessary changes or develop a new plan of recognition that more effectively honors the diverse needs of our people both individually and collectively.

The study of opposites can be intriguing as well as profoundly integrating. We begin with the premise that opposites are complimentary, not contradictory. The whole, or unity, is composed of and only exists when it contains what at first appear to be opposites. For example, take the concepts of pain and pleasure. If we really understand what life is about, we begin to see that there is no real difference between pain and pleasure. Think of the ocean. You don't look at the ocean and see the crest and the trough. What you see is the combination of the crest and the trough, which we call a wave. It is not the UP that is important to make it a wave, and it is not the DOWN. What is important is the up and down together—that makes the ebb and flow. And this is true in our lives as well. There is no fall without the spring and no spring without the fall. Light must have darkness as day must have night. Neither are better. Each concept only exists by contrast. We can see ourselves better when we notice ourselves in terms of the opposites—or the contrasts that exist within and between us.

Let's look at an example. I have a very close friend who works with people who have been diagnosed with AIDS. She dedicates her whole life to this. She takes people in, they live with her, and she watches them die. Luckily, she has been blessed with a healthy husband and two beautiful, healthy children. Recently, she confided in me that she was ready to give up her work with these people. She said, "I can't do this anymore. It's draining me, it's draining my life." When I asked her what would be the opposite of what she was doing, she began to realize that the contrast of living so closely to death each day was what helped her see the beauty of her life that much more. She suddenly saw the gift of her life with her family because she'd seen the pain and suffering. Rainbows are only possible when it's rained!

The opposites that we think we see in life are amazing. We talk about children and adults. Increasingly, books, articles, and lectures are leading us all to discover that we are both. Do you experience the child in you? Or do you have no adult at all? That's something we want to look at in the office or the boardroom. Are we playing to the child? Or are we taking ourselves so seriously, playing at being the adult all the time? We are all both, so as a manager, as a motivator, we must appeal to both parts in others. I've seen companies who have what first appears to be the silliest recognition programs, like dressing up as clowns, or giving out teddy bears, work like a charm. The kid in all of us needs to be recognized as well!

And then there is the dimension of male and female within each of us. There is a great deal being written today about gender differences. We might not think of the male and female difference when we are looking at how to recognize people. There is very little research done to date on this topic. But, if it is true that males prefer to be recognized one way and females another, what about the part of each of us that is male or female regardless of our physical makeup or sexual orientation?

We also need to consider, for example, what energy is produced by a female manager with male employees or male managers with female employees. This doesn't necessarily mean sexual energy—although that does play a part, but there's a world to explore out there about gender differences and how that effects the way we recognize and motivate others. I simply raise the issue here because it's one of the opposites that we seldom discuss in the workplace. I have observed that men usually recognize other men's work or ideas and most often give recognition to women for their appearance. Women are equally the culprits, recognizing other women, but seldom recognizing men. It's an issue worth pondering—and changing.

Another opposite polarity that I believe we all deal with frequently is the swing between being caring and apathetic. The best of us are loving and avoiding, giving and taking at the same time. At times we are caring and lots of times we couldn't care less. What makes us choose one over the other? Some say the answer is in our constitution—the way our genes get thrown together. Others say it's in the environment. If you live with something all the time you may begin to be like that or you may become the opposite.

There are all kinds of studies being done lately on adult children of alcoholics. There is a classic story about two sons of an alcoholic who met one day. One lived in squalor and was drinking heavily and the other was a successful, sober businessman. When the son who was drinking was asked, "Why are you drinking?," he said, "Because my father did." And when the other son was asked, "Why don't you drink?," he said, "Because my father did."

It's all perspective—it's in the way you view the world. As in all differences, in all dualities, we tend to choose one over the other. Therefore, our understanding only caters to half of the population—to half of our employees—at best. These opposites affect the way we manage, the way we learn, and the way we give and receive recognition.

Some people thrive on change. Others resist it at all costs. In one government logistics environment, the manager works with his change-resistant employees by introducing new ideas as challenges—they love to solve puzzles. So, this encourages them to actively pursue the new idea.

Another pair of differences you'll often find in the workplace is whether someone is process-oriented or product-oriented. Are you working with people or getting a product produced? What is the thing you are concentrating on right now? Certain people will lean towards a more logical lets-get-it-done mode and others will be more involved in how people are getting on, or how are they responding in the department, division, organization, or company. Both are important. Years of research on types of leadership have shown this over and over again. In the early 1900s, Frederick Winslow Taylor introduced the scientific management theory that focused on technology. Because people were viewed as instruments, the best way to increase productivity was to improve techniques and develop more efficient administrators. In the 1920s and early 1930s, Elton Mayo and others introduced the human relations movement. They argued that the real power leaders were those who understood human nature and who could effect positive interpersonal relations within the workplace. There are no conclusive studies that one philosophy is more effective than the other. Most of the latest theories have come to combine these views. Both types of staff members and leaders exist in our organizations. Failure to understand these differences wastes a great deal of time and energy. It is not appropriate to argue which style works best. The leader of tomorrow will be able to understand his or her own style as well as learn to recognize, acknowledge, and appreciate those who are different.

Some people will always be more objective, while others are more subjective. Some are more analytic, others more personal. Some are right-brained and creative and others more left-brained, linear, and logical. For those who like the personal touch, it is important to be acknowledged for being someone adept at dealing with people. Getting the project done on time is secondary! And, of course, for their counterparts, a 180° opposite approach is better.

How well have you noticed any of these differences in the past? You don't have to get an MBA to see them. The first step is AWARENESS. For those who are already aware: How have you applied this to the way you recognize and motivate people? Are you aware of differences but still treating people as if they are all the same?

NEURO-LINGUISTIC PROGRAMMING

Metaprograms

We have much to learn about opposites and about differences in general from the science of neuro-linguistic programming (NLP). NLP is a study of how the nervous system (neuro) and brain are conditioned through language (linguistic) and experience to make meaning out of life's events. It was created by Richard Bandler and John Grinder in the 1970s and a form of it, which is called Neuro Associative Conditioning, has been recently popularized by Tony Robbins in his best sellers, *Unlimited Power* (Simon & Schuster, 1986) and *Awaken the Giant Within* (Summit Books, 1991). It is ultimately a study of the biochemical and electrical learning (called imprinting) of our nervous systems. From this, we can learn a great deal about how we learn and how our brains associate meaning.

One of the concepts that NLP teaches is how to discover your own or someone else's metaprograms. Metaprograms are the specific ways we delete or filter out certain experiences while letting others into our lives. They are the internal sorting mechanism we use to decide to what we will give our attention. Metaprograms are not static. They depend on your state of being at the time and on the specific context or stress of your life. We'll be discussing how to elicit a few of the metaprograms. The ones I have chosen to discuss will better help us to understand how to uniquely recognize our employees by studying their behavior at a particular time and circumstance. Each metaprogram can be viewed as a continuum. Some people's specific behavior will favor one end of the continuum, while others will favor the other. And then, some behaviors seem to fall equally in the middle.

Moving Toward—Moving Away

We can discover if someone is using a moving toward or a moving away from strategy simply by asking a question like, What do you want in a relationship? Or in a job? Or in a leader? They will either answer with a word or list of what they are looking for, or else they will answer with what they are looking to avoid. You'll hear many people answer questions like these by beginning, "Well, I know what I DON'T want." Or, "Let me tell you what leadership is NOT."

When you seem to be getting a moving toward response from someone, that is the time to motivate them with possibilities. If a person's answer fits more of a moving away mode, the best reply to them will be to suggest how they can avoid something. It's really very simple, yet so few people know how to use it to advantage.

Matchers—Mismatchers

There are people who at certain times tend to notice how alike things are. In this instance, they can be described as *matchers.* People who notice how different things are, can be described as *mismatchers.* Notice, this is not a label we put on people at all times, in all circumstances. It is a behavior at a given time that we are noticing.

Stop reading for a moment and throw three coins of the same denomination randomly on a table. What do you observe? Some of you will describe the coins and talk about the fact that they are all made of the *same* metal. Some of you will talk about how the three coins are *different* from each other perhaps in position or some irregularity of their shape. Some of us are oriented toward differences, some of us are oriented toward sameness. Be careful not to jump to the conclusion that someone is being negative when what they are simply doing is processing information as a mismatcher. If you are managing people who are difference oriented, you ought to be motivating them by telling them how things can be different. If you manage people who are sameness oriented, you ought to be motivating them by having them notice how what you want is like something they already want. There's a challenge here; one set of people is motivated in one way, another set is exactly opposite, and the real masterful motivators are people who know and can utilize each person's preference to complete advantage. We need to learn to express things differently for different people. We can find out if someone is matching or mismatching in their need for recognition by asking a question such as, "How well do you feel recognized on this project as compared with the one you did last week (or year or job)?"

Internal—External

You can elicit a person's internal or external frame of reference by asking a question like, "How do you know when you've done something well?" The person who's frame is internal will tell you about how they feel inside or what they tell themselves, while a person who has an external reference frame usually answers, "I know because someone tells me."

Yet, if a person says they "know when someone tells them," wouldn't it stand to reason then that they need to HEAR when and if they are doing a good job? What will motivate them is being told. How many ways can you find to tell someone their work is good? If you are working from an internal reference, you may be unaware of another person's need to get feedback. The tendency many of us have is to say, "They shouldn't need to hear it. They should KNOW when they are doing a good job." Beliefs like this can be dangerous. Once again, we are assuming that everyone is just the same as we are, and moreover, if they are not, they SHOULD be!

Even the person who is working more from an internal reference may need to have a mirror to reflect from. Some may need to tell you about what they have done, so that they can hear it themselves. When we discuss personality later in this chapter, we'll see that about 75% of the population has this need. Even those who usually have an internal reference when doing what they feel comfortable with, when it comes to a new project or working relationship, they may, in that instance, have more of a need for external input.

You can see, these notions are dynamic—like people themselves. Remember that metaprograms are not meant to define and pigeonhole people for all times and in all circumstances. We don't want to limit a person and generalize. In this specific context, they are exhibiting an internal or external strategy. Beware of making quick judgments about a person based on the answer to one question! Assume nothing. Ask questions often.

Possibility—Necessity

When we ask a person why they do something, we can discover a great deal about whether they are motivated by possibility or necessity. "Why do you stay at this job?," for example, will tell you a great deal about how to motivate this person. If he says, "Because I need the money," and she says, "Because I think there's a chance I can get into a sales position," you now have a good sense of how each wants to be recognized.

Global—Detail

NLP often speaks of "chunking things down or up." When we refer to chunk size, we are looking at whether a person is taking a global or a detailed view. If a person wants and needs to know the big picture, they are seeing things from a global perspective. The person who likes the specifics and logistics before getting to the overall view is more of a detail oriented thinker. We'll talk about this at length when we discuss personality types.

Internal Representations

In addition to looking at opposites, NLP also teaches us about representational systems, which for our purposes are yet another way of understanding differences. There are several processes by which we select what it is we will see. So much data comes to us daily through sight, sound, smell, touch, and taste. We cannot pay attention to all of it, so our brains go through a selection process and create psychological maps from part of the data. A. Korzybski, a semanticist and linguist who wrote *Science and Sanity* in 1933, gave the term "territory" to the external world and labeled the way that we represent the world of our experience, "the map of the territory." He made an important distinction, which once again underlines that perception is not reality, when he said, "a map is not the territory it represents, but, if correct, it has a similar structure to the territory, which accounts for its usefulness." Our behaviors are based on what has been selected, our representation of the world we experience through our senses. We all have preferences when it comes to perceiving the world. Knowing people's predominant "map", model of the world, or internal representational system can be extremely helpful in understanding the way they can best see, hear, or feel recognized.

There are several sensory components of our maps. Internally, we see pictures and images, which NLP labels the visual-internal mode (V-i), and hear inner dialogue or self-talk, labeled auditory-internal mode (A-i). When you think about your office or your desk at work, you'd create a picture in your imagination to see it. You may also have conversations with yourself about it that could be favorable or not depending on your feelings about your work and your ability to organize. When you add feelings or emotions (kinesthetics or K-i) to the pictures and words, you begin to "make meaning."

Some people seem to operate from a more visual perspective. They map their psychological world in terms of pictures. Others are auditory and they map their world from sounds or tones. Kinesthetics are most comfortable both with the sense of touch and with internal feelings.

You can begin to practice finding someone's representational system by listening to the predominant words used in conversation. You will find visuals saying things like: I see, look, view, show, envision, and imagine. It is clear, foggy. It appears. (You get the picture!). You will "hear" auditory words that include: hear, harmonize, sounds like, rings a bell, resonate, question, and listen. (Am I making myself clear?) And you'll "get a sense of" the Kinesthetic's vocabulary from words like: touch, feel, get hold of, tap into, make contact, get a handle, hard, and unfeeling. (Are you beginning to "grasp" what I mean?)

When someone says, "It *appears to me* that *in light of* this well-defined *view*, we are still not *seeing eye to eye*." There is no doubt that they are coming from a high visual mode. Remember that the first step of recognition is awareness and it would be counterproductive to answer that person with, "To *tell the truth*, I've *heard* you *word for word describe every detail*, but I'm *telling* you, *loud and clear*, that there are *hidden messages* here that we need to *inquire into*." What it all *boils down to*, is that both need to *get in touch* with the fact that they are not *getting the drift*, and are not *standing on a firm foundation*. They must start from *scratch* to *get a handle* on the real *feelings* underlying the words.

Highly visual representations include fast speech, high chest breathing, high pitched, sometimes nasal voices, and muscle tension in the shoulders and abdomen. A more modulated tone, balanced tempo, clear, resonant, pleasing to listen to tone might belong more to the auditory mode. Breathing is usually deeper into the diaphragm and the person often folds his or her hands or arms, with the head tilted slightly to one side as if to listen more intently. The kinesthetic mode is a slower tempo, more pauses, and deeper tonality usually accompanied by a lot of body movement externally but with internal muscles relaxed. The head is often square on the shoulders.

When we learn a person's dominant representational systems, we move a long way towards understanding HOW they want appreciation shown. Recognition is about being SEEN, HEARD, and UNDERSTOOD. Although all of these are important for all of us, for some people, one part of the equation needs more emphasis than the other parts for the recognition sent to be the recognition received.

Visuals

We might simply say things like, "I see your point" or "I want you to take a look at this," to let the person know you are AWARE. To thank them, you need to SHOW them they are appreciated. Acknowledge them for the way things look, for their appearance, for creating an atmosphere. This type of person wants something they can SEE, like a written note. Or, if they are externally oriented, they may want something that other people can see, like a story or picture in the company newsletter.

Auditory

"I hear what you are saying," can be some of the most affirming words you can use with an auditory. "I need your advice; Does this sound right to you?" Now, you are resonating with their need for being heard. Wouldn't it make sense, then, that an auditory likes to hear what they have done well? They want the verbal thank you and sometimes the word spoken in front of their peers. They like to be acknowledged as people who speak well or who really listen to others and understand.

Kinesthetic

Tell a kinesthetic that their work is "rock solid" or that they "really have a grasp or a handle on the situation" and you have made their day. Give them any written or verbal clue that it doesn't *feel* right to you and you've done the opposite.

A kinesthetic approach includes internal feelings as well as tactile, concrete expressions. Show appreciation with a hug (where appropriate) or with something they can touch or keep on their desk and "play with." Kinesthetics actually learn by using their keen sense of touch as well.

Think about the married couple who continue to argue. "But I tell you all the time how much I love you." "Yes, but, you never buy me things, you never take me places, you don't *show* me." It's a classic case of mixed-matched representational systems that could be so easily resolved by noticing that we are so used to giving love the way we want to receive it, rather than the way it can best be received. Or, think of the boss who says things like "It just doesn't feel right to me" and the puzzled employees turn to each other, "Did you hear what he said?" "I don't see what she means." Communication is the art of being understood. The meaning is not in the message being sent, but in the response that is elicited. What we send out as love, is not really felt as love, until the receiver perceives it as such. It's a thought worth pondering.

TYPOLOGY

Another method of understanding differences makes use of personality type. There are many different systems of organizing and dividing personalities. For the sake of simplicity and illustration, we'll only discuss three.

Stanford Research Model—VALS

The first is a psychographic model developed by Stanford Research Institute. This model came from a study to discover the driving force behind human behavior in the US. It divides people into five categories: belongers, emulators, achievers, societal conscious, and need driven.

A belonger is a person whose number one value is having a sense of family, or belonging. These are the people who believe in motherhood and apple pie and comprise approximately 38% of the population. A belonger wants most to be praised for being a "team player" or an outstanding company employee. These are the people who also love to wear company jackets and T-shirts and their desks and homes are adorned with company paraphernalia that represent the traditional mode of recognition. Belongers also are more appreciative of "breakfasts with the boss" or other functions where they get to be a part of things.

Emulators want more than anything else to experience confidence to create material success. About 20% of the population fall into this category. These people are not impressed with low-cost items even if they are meant to say "great job." What they want to know is how they are doing relative to where they want to get in the company. What are their chances of meeting their financial goals, and how soon can they expect to reach them? Many high-producing sales people are in this category. They thrive on commission because they feel they are being compensated in accordance to the work they produce. They cannot be stopped by a financial glass ceiling. They feel recognized when their names are shown on the winning charts.

Achievers, about 18% of the population, value uniqueness above everything else. They'd buy something instantly if they were convinced it was one of a kind. They like to be singled out for doing or being something that no one else has done or been. They dress differently; you'll find the unusual artifacts in their office. In fact, if you want to show them that you appreciate them, bring them back a "one of a kind" artwork or piece of jewelry from an exotic trip. Compliment them by saying how different their approach to a problem is or how unique a solution they've discovered.

Societal-conscious people comprise about 22% of the population and intelligence is what is most important to them. Their ideas are more important than anything else. It is not necessary to make a fanfare banquet or ceremony for these people. Simply USE their ideas. They are even insulted if you compliment them too much; they EXPECT themselves to be excellent and only need an occasional affirmation of that excellence.

The last 2% of the population are driven purely by survival. These are people who live on government assistance and are fearful of dying and leaving their family without resources. When someone is struggling with basic needs, help fill their basic needs.

Achievement—Power—Affiliation

Another way we can look at differences in people is to note which drives them more—achievement, power, or affiliation.

Achievement

Those with high achievement needs seek lots of feedback when doing a job. They are not comfortable until a job is completed and work best when there is a deadline. A way of recognizing them is to give them more challenging work or added responsibility. They always set high standards of performance, so they do not like "light" compliments. Achievers do, however, tend to be competitive, so traditional "races for rewards" would please them and motivate them to accomplish more.

David McClelland and his associates at Harvard have studied this compulsion to achieve for the last 20 or so years. He noted that achievers set reachable goals that stretch their current ability. They like to play it safe. Acknowledge achievers, then, by making certain that they can influence the outcome of any project in which they are involved. They like to know the effect of their efforts and abilities, so it is important to let them know, even though they are less concerned than most with outward awards. Although they accept the external kudos of their peers, their real reward is a personal sense of accomplishment. Praise them by giving them yet another—perhaps bigger—problem to solve or contest to win. Money can be a measurement of performance, but it is not their exclusive reward.

People with a high need for achievement usually place themselves in situations in which they can get concrete feedback on their progress. Obviously, the nature of the feedback would be important as well. This type of person likes to keep score. They are on target with quality goals of "always trying to find a better way of doing things." Achievement-oriented people usually get more raises and are promoted faster because of this. They are highly task-oriented and expect others to be as well. They want to know how well they are doing with their ideas, or with the actual work accomplished and would be less motivated by praise on how much of a team player they are or any other personal characteristic. The one major drawback they have in an organization that is focused on quality, is that they have a tendency to be more independent and have a more difficult time as managers of people—especially of people who may be different from themselves.

Affiliation

On the other hand, people motivated by affiliation needs want social feedback. They thrive on hearing about how their attitude or personableness contributed to the success of a project. They place a high value on harmonious relationships and usually are attentive to people's needs and wants because they also want to feel needed and wanted. People with high affiliation needs like to be praised for being team players. They love group projects. In fact, they do not like to work alone. At the heart of the need for affiliation is the desire to have our beliefs validated and confirmed. All of us join groups with people like ourselves, but some of us have greater social needs than others.

Recognition that comes in the form of being given work we love to do is sometimes the most rewarding. People with high affiliation needs go out of their way to make friends with someone who is new. So, one way of recognizing this is to assign them to that task. You could also call upon an affiliator to be a reconciler, because they like to help others. But, at extremes, affiliators may want too much to be approved and liked, so may take less risks or be less honest in a situation that calls for assertive confrontation.

Sometimes affiliation needs may be temporary. For example, if a previously strong relationship has been shattered, or a person leaves a prevailing belief system, he or she would want to associate with others who have the new belief in order for his or her own doubt to be dissipated. Like recognition, we all need some external validation for our beliefs.

Power

Power is a our potential to have others comply or be influenced by what we say, do, or believe. Power can be positional, as in the case of a director, boss, military commander, or parent. It can also be personal, based on charismatic personal qualities.

For our purposes here, we might simply consider power as synonymous with influence. A person who is motivated more by influence than by achievement or affiliation usually prefers to work alone and not be told what to do. If this person happens to work for you, recognize them by giving few global directions and a lot of leeway to work independently.

They like status symbols, so trophies, awards, and plaques may be the way to go—IF, in fact, these symbolize power in your organization. Sometimes, power is symbolized by the location of an office, or the height of the dividers around their workspace. Each place of work has its own symbols of power and they probably are quite evident when we allow ourselves to recognize them.

These people can often be recognized by titles as well, as long as the title comes with the authority to do the job and be in charge, even if it is of a single event or project. Ask for the ideas of power-motivated people and be sure to use them as well. Especially acknowledge their ideas about how to influence change in other people. They are usually verbally fluent, so allow these people to publicly express their opinions as well.

Be sure you have neutralized the effect of the word *power* in your own mind. Many people judge others who seem to need and want status and influence. Alfred Adler, the psychologist who introduced the concepts of inferiority complex and compensation taught us a great deal about power. People who have had difficulty as children because of their position, with parents who wanted excessive control, may have grown up feeling inadequate about winning the admiration and respect of others. They may either shy away completely, or demand it. Either of these attitudes could be what prevails behind a manager's behavior that is overbearing or power-hungry.

On the other hand, if a person grows through the normal feeling of childhood powerlessness in a mature fashion, he or she will transform that need for power into a desire to perfect social relationships. This person will make an excellent manager, because in their concern for power, their concentration will be on how to influence relationships so that a greater degree of trust and respect develops. We need managers and leaders who have this ability and desire.

No one type is better than another. The point is, they all exist. At times, each of the above designations may exist in each of us. Our lives are dynamic and changing, and so our motives may also adapt and change as well. Recognition is challenging, because we are constantly aiming at a moving target!

Jung's Typology and the MBTI

One difference that changes less readily (and in fact, which some psychologists—like C.J. Jung—don't believe change at all), is our personality type. This next section discusses a particular system of personality typing. I've chosen to discuss the Jungian classifications in greater depth because, after all of my research on this topic, I still find it to be the richest system. The more I learn about it, the more I discover in it—and that's after 15 years!

In looking at representational systems, we addressed *how* people like to receive recognition. We study personality types to start to notice different types of behaviors and needs to know *what* people want to be acknowledged for. We can then begin a process of learning to recognize people in the way that would be uniquely special to each one.

When you learn to be sensitive to behaviors in others, you come to know that it's very important to be more logical and clear and give specific detailed directions for some people to best hear what you are saying. Recognition for that person would include more specifics. And for someone else, it's important to give the big picture before you get to the how or the details. These people want recognition for their ideas—and most want their ideas used, not just talked about.

If you are a new manager, or just new to personality differences, some of this might seem overwhelming. When I teach managers about unique recognition of individuals, I know they have understood all that is involved in this when they begin to say, "It's impossible to think of all of this stuff at once." And, they are right. It is. But after a while, it becomes almost second nature—somewhat like driving a car. I don't consciously think about what personality type is this person so how should I respond? Occasionally, I need to make it more conscious when I notice something isn't working. It's like any new skill, when you are first learning it you need to concentrate more on it and then it becomes second nature. And, for the veteran, even old skills sometimes need revisiting and sometimes revising.

You can start by noticing who you pay attention to in your office. Most people like people who are like them. We don't join clubs with people who are different. And, we tend to recognize the work of people who work like we do. This may seem obvious, but listen to the comments of people (purposely left anonymous) from various organizations (also anonymous) from around the country who don't feel recognized:

> Until recently, much of the internal communication in my organization was unresponsive to its intended audience. Management told employees what the employees should think and feel, and how they should act. Employees responded by ignoring management communication. I felt neglected, and ignored. I don't think anyone knows who I really am around here.

> Essentially, it doesn't feel as though anyone cares if we come to work or not. Most of us never even hear the words, "job well done." I need to hear how I am doing more often, not just when it is time for performance appraisal. My performance is important to me and I know I do good work, but gosh, no one else seems to know.

> There is no adequate feedback. Goal setting, employee empowerment, these are nice words, but they are all missing. I want to be recognized for being competent. I don't want someone over my shoulder telling me what to do. Or, some-

one patting me on the back all of the time either. Excellent work speaks for itself.

Programs or promises are either inconsistently applied or are not followed up. These certainly act as demotivators. I want concrete expressions that say I belong here. I can show them specific facts and details of what I've done. Why can't the recognition be concrete as well?

What we have represented here are very different needs, expressed differently by different personalities. You may not have the luxury to take personality inventories of your staff, but you can take the time to ask them some questions. One of the best ways of finding out how different people like to be recognized is to ask them! When was the last time you asked that of the people who work for you, with you, or even above you? Be careful with this. One of the things people often say when asked a question is "I don't know." People do know. If they don't, who does? One of the ways to respond to this is to ask, "Well, what would you say if you did know?" It is amazing what our brains know when encouraged. People do know what is best for them, what they most want, and eventually, if they believe you sincerely want to know—and this is crucial—they will respond. When people are allowed to be themselves, where they are, and who they are, they get far more work done.

We need to do a lot of self-analysis and know ourselves to be able to do this well, and be sure that we are not imposing ourselves on our employees. Once I am attuned to who I am and how I am motivated and therefore probably the way I motivate others, then I can start to open my eyes and say, "Oh, there are other people out there." How well do you know the people who work for you? Do you know what their number-one values are? Are you continually updating that information?

I am asking you to be sensitized. First to yourself, and then to the people around you. So learn your own personality preferences and by inference, the way you are best motivated or recognized. Be aware of leading from an unexamined impulse. We can learn to be better motivators by being better self-witnesses. I always want to be aware of where and what my own preferences are, so I can become more conscious of what I do naturally and then learn to notice when a different behavior is needed. Self-knowledge is the first step to changing. As I recognize that all my preferences create my reality, I'll learn to become more creative as a motivator and as a person as well.

There is a whole other world out there. There are people who see things very, very differently than you do and they are not wrong—they are just different. And isn't it true in life that the people who are the most successful are simply the ones that recognize more options?

When I begin asking people about their personality types, someone will say, "It depends—when I'm at work I'm one thing, when I'm home I'm another." I think it is a sad state of affairs when we cannot be ourselves at work. What does it say about what behavior gets rewarded? I never thought some of my behavior was okay, simply because it was different from the way others around me were doing things. When I learned that I was simply being true to my type, I became more comfortable in expressing my self—as myself—while fully alert to the fact that my type represents only 16% of the population, and would therefore appear to be different. It takes courage to be ourselves in a work setting where sameness is often prized. But the rewards to ourselves and our companies are great when we are all offering who we are at the highest level. Productivity cannot help but increase. I'm not saying that we should use type as an excuse to do things our own way. All of us, as integrated adults, can choose the behavior appropriate to the moment. In fact, learning about who we are makes us more conscious of when we have the need for a different person and another way of looking at situations.

Personality evolves as we start exercising our preferences. One thing becomes more important than the other, and sometimes we get rewarded for one kind of behavior over another. There are lots of theories about how personality develops. Is it nature or nurture? Jung claims it is latent in our genes but is not genetically inherited. Many people are the total opposite of their parents. It's an absolute miracle that my personality developed as it did. My father keeps shaking his head, "I don't know why your way works, but it seems to work for you." As an adult, I am getting that recognition. When I was a kid, it was not easy to be what I will later explain is an ENFP. I was a sensitive, feeling child who liked exploring new things. And my parents are very structured and orderly—a place for everything and everything in its place. Life is simple for them; you go to work for 35 years and then you retire. When I told them I was quitting a good job they said, "You're committing the crime of a century. You have a high-paying job, why would you ever give up all that security?" I said "Security? That's no fun." I have a very different value system.

I spent a good deal of my life thinking that it wasn't OK to be who I was, it was more OK to be a different kind of person. Personality development certainly isn't just genes. My parents lean toward one edge and my sister and I lean toward the opposite edge. I look at my sister's now grown twins; they have different likes, dislikes, and personality types, but they're twins. They were born at the same time to the same parents and raised in the same environment, so there has to be another explanation.

The history of personality theory goes back to 1921 and the Swiss psychoanalyst, Carl Jung. He described his study of the psychological types. He noted that there were two major functions in the way our brains operate. Jung was that first to recognize that people make clear choices from infancy on how they will use their minds. He divided the functions into two pairs of opposites or polarities. Like our natural preference for being right or left handed, Jung proposed that we have psychological preferences as well. If we look at the way people behave, it is not really random. There are clear patterns. He classified personalities according to their perception and judgment functions and originated the concepts of extraversion and introversion, concepts that have remained basic building blocks of personality theory.

One of the things he noticed is the way people take in data from the outside world; the way they look at things. Jung said that people see the world in one of two ways. Some people see the world exactly as it is. They see the details in front of them, and are very concrete. If someone were to take a chair and pick it up in anger, what would they see? They would see the legs, the arms, the seat, the color, or the other parts and then see me pick it up—that is, seeing what is. These people are sensing perceivers— they take in information in parts, perceiving fine details according to the five senses. Most of the world "sees" this way. In fact, research has shown it to be about 75%.

Other people perceive the world in its entirety rather than piecemeal. In the scene above, they would see an angry person about to throw something at someone. They would see possibilities—what could happen, rather than what is actually happening. This is another way of looking at things—by interpretations, implications, and possibilities for the future. Jung called this intuition. I wish he hadn't used the word intuition, because today it is overused and, of course everyone can learn to use intuition more effectively. But, this is not what he is talking about. He is referring to the way we perceive—very concretely or very abstractly. We see either what is or what can be. And so, for Jung, the opposite of sensing perception is intuitive perception.

Sensors are interested in facts; they tend to focus their attention on details; they look at exactly what is. Intuitors on the other hand, are interested in ideas, they focus attention on the future . . . seeing what could be, soaring to new heights. Sensors are interested in doing things that have immediate practical use. They are comfortable with a standard way of doing things, while intuitors are interested in possibilities. They prefer generating ideas rather than being responsible for putting them into action. Occasionally, when details become too complicated, sensors want to make things as simple as possible. The intuitor on the other hand, would complicate things. They trust inspiration, vision, and imagination. Sensors believe that practice makes perfect. They trust hard work and perspiration. Intuitors prefer metaphors and elaboration. Sensors enjoy using skills that they've already learned rather than learning new ones. They can work steadily with realistic ideas of how long something will take. And they like getting things done as quickly as possible. Intuitors like to learn new skills more than using them. They work in bursts of energy, empowered with enthusiasm with slack periods in between. And they work continuously when they are interested in what they are doing.

After you take in information, how do you process it? Jung describes this as our second major function. People process information in one of two opposite ways—either you are a thinking judger or a feeling judger. We have to define those pretty carefully because these words also don't signify what they are commonly accepted to mean. Different words for these might be "analytical" for thinker and "belief-oriented" for feeler persons. We are talking about how somebody makes a decision, how a person evaluates and judges data. He called this the judging function. You can make decisions based on cause and effect:

"This is true, and this is true, therefore this is true." Thinkers process or judge data in a formalized, linear fashion and can be described as logical. Feelers, on the other hand, are people who make decisions or judgments on what is important, what is of value to them, and how the decision will affect others. Thinkers make decisions based on principles. Feelers make a decision based on a process that more closely reflects personal values. They seem to be subtilely different. You can come up with exactly the same result making decisions either way. It is the *process* of decision making that is incredibly different.

Thinkers make decisions impersonally, based on logical analysis. Things have to have a solid foundation. They have to figure things out before they take action. Feelers, on the other hand, make all decisions based on personal feelings . . . responding to their own likes and dislikes. And they tend to act on personal feelings. Thinkers exhibit consistent and predictable behavior . . . very traditional. Feelers tend to be more spontaneous—they may be way up or way down. They work in a seemingly scattered, messy, and unorganized manner. Thinkers are interested in work that is neat, orderly, and well-organized. Thinkers are interested in detailed factual information. They like charts, graphs, and maps. To feelers, everything has to have a more personal meaning. A thinker is often independent of other people. Where feelers seek approval, thinkers need to be treated fairly. They like to keep things balanced and sometimes may seem hard-hearted. Feelers, on the other hand, need praise. They enjoy pleasing people. They enjoy harmony. Thinkers rely on their organizational skills, and they tend to be objective. Everything has a place. Feelers, on the other hand, rely on relational skills. They tend to be sympathetic . . . everything has a meaning.

You may began to wonder "How do people ever communicate?" Imagine being married to somebody when you are making a decision one way and they are making a decision in the opposite way? Or working with a supervisor who doesn't even perceive things as you do? Understanding personality theory will help you go a long way in learning how to communicate more effectively.

Everyone has both a perceiving function (sensing, which is referred to as "S" or intuition, which is labeled with an "N"—we will be using "I" for introversion later on). So, thus far, we can start combining and see that we already have determined that you can be a: sensing-thinker (ST), a sensing-feeler (SF), an intuitive-thinker (NT), or an intuitive-feeler (NF).

Within the same perceiving function, people are very different. You can have two sensors but if you have a sensing-thinker (ST) you have a very different person from a sensing-feeler (SF). SFs are people you want around when you are sick; they are going to bring you chicken soup. They are very practical people who are also very caring. STs are out there into the details and the reality of the moment; they use their sensing skills more with projects than with people. The ST would probably analyze what you need and tell you. Within the judging function (either thinking or feeling), the intuitive-thinker (NT) also has a very logical mind, but instead of focusing on the concrete details of the here and now, the NT would be analyzing the great models and theories of the world while creating some of their own. Meanwhile, the intuitive-feeler (NF) is the one who spends time and energy caring and worrying about how all of these theories and models will affect humankind. So, just by combining the two functions you can begin to see the nuances of different personality types. Knowing that a person has a preference for ST, SF, NT, or NF tells you a great deal about their behavior patterns as well as about the way they need to be recognized.

Jung also studied what he called the "attitudes" we have towards life. He taught that people are introverted or extroverted, depending on their source of energy. Some people need people and interaction around them even to know what they are thinking. We could say that extroverts (E) don't even know what they are thinking until they hear themselves say it. Energy comes to them from the outside in. When they are trying to make a decision, they have to call seven friends and talk it out. They don't necessarily want someone else to give them an answer. They don't want someone to tell them what they should do . . . they simply need to hear themselves speak to think. The more they speak, the clearer their own thinking gets.

Other people get all of their energy from their internal world. These people he labeled introverts (I). Be careful with this word. This does not mean a person is a wallflower, so quiet and shy that you can't talk to them. This does not mean that they are antisocial. An introvert, according to Jung, is someone whose energy comes from their own internal world of ideas—from the inside out. After an introvert spends time alone, they reappear energized. Note that we are not saying that introverts do not relate well to others. They can do any or all of the same things an extravert might do, their energy source is just different. For example, either extroverts or introverts may be great on a stage. They may both become great public speakers. See what's happening here? It is important to rethink the kind of associations you may have had to these words. We are not talking about the things you do well, we are talking about your preferences, and in this case, your energy source; what empowers you to go on. Is it talking about it, is it verbalizing it, or is interacting with other people and working with other objects? Or is what goes on in your internal world that energizes you? This is one of Jung's most significant contributions.

One of the things to notice with an introvert is that when they are asked a question, they usually look down and often close their eyes. It's almost like they are looking inside to find the answer. Those who are extroverted tend to be caught up in someone else's enthusiasm. Extroverts get and need their feedback from the world. Sometimes people who are extroverted don't even know they have done a good job unless someone tells them.

We will spend the rest of this chapter working on understanding these combined personality differences. Once you figure out who you are, you can reread and apply all of this to recognition—particularly learning WHAT each person wants to be acknowledged for.

Jung's theory was taken one step further and popularized through what has come to be known as the Myers-Briggs Type Indicator (MBTI). Its authors were two women, mother and daughter, Catherine Briggs and Isabel Briggs-Myers. Catherine was creating her own theory of personality type around the time that Jung did his writing. Her interest in personality differences started when her daughter, Isabel, brought home her future husband, a man who was so "different" from the rest of the family.

Although she had no formal education, Catherine arrived at a theory that codified some 40 factors of personality with charts and observations. She developed the instrument by tallying the results of all her neighbors and all her friends. She started noting that there were clear differences. When she read Jung, she discovered somebody who validated what she believed in. To help this theory reach the largest number of people, she dedicated her life to creating a paper and pencil instrument so people could assess themselves and discover their true type. Because she and her daughter were both intuitive-feeler types (and for an NF, everything has to have a meaning and a purpose), they decided that what Jung was presenting could help put an end to war. The year was 1945. Peace in the world was what they were after. They sat down and studied a lot of people. They got permission to go into schools and kept creating and discarding questions until they found ones that would remain consistent over time and type. Isabel would use her husband, who was her exact opposite and ask, "What do you think of this question?" At first, that is how the instrument was developed. Over the years, it became more formalized. Much to their credit, not being psychologists and not being people who worked with tests and measurements, they honed a very precise instrument. They later added a section of word pairs, which could further cross-check the validity of a person's answers. Eventually, they were able to convince the Educational Testing Service in New Jersey to take over the instrument and do extensive research, thereby refining the instrument in terms of statistical validity and reliability.

While they were refining the instrument, they added to Jung's theory. They noticed that, not only do people use the four functions of sensing, intuiting, thinking, and feeling, but they also have a preference within the functions either for perceiving (S or N) or for judging (T or F). Think of the decision-making process. To make a good decision, we should use all four of these functions. First, we collect the data (S). Once the data has been collected, we abstract the implications and possibilities contained within that data (N). This is the perceiving part. Next, we judge the data. We make a logical decision based on the implications of that data (T). We then conclude the process by observing what effect it will have and how it will affect any people involved (F). During our personal decision-making or group processes, most of us concentrate our efforts only on the functions that we prefer. Some of us concentrate on collecting data, and some of us concentrate on seeing the implications. Some of us make all of our decisions by spending most of the allotted decision-making time collecting facts whether the facts are concrete evidence or abstractions. Others of us make the decision the most important step, whether or not we have gathered all of the data. "This is right; or, this is going to make everybody happy, I just know it."

Of the two functions in each of our preferences, we all have one that is dominant. Those for whom the most important and exciting part of the process is collecting data are dominant-perceivers (i.e., they are either S or N dominant). Those who get to the decision as quickly as possible are dominant-judgers (i.e., they are either T or F dominant). Which is more important to you? Taking in information (perceiving) or making a decision on information (judging)? We can now add the letters P or J, based on which of the functions are most important to you. This one is a life-style implication. Is it more important to keep gathering information? Do you not care if you ever make a decision? Do you like to go and check out all the possibilities? Usually, then, you are a more laid back, easygoing, come-what-may type (P). Or, do you make checklists so that everything will get done? Does everything have a time and a place? Are you uncomfortable unless a decision has been made (J)?

Let me tell you how I once bought a car. I needed it soon, so it had to be in stock. I wanted it close to my house, because my theory was if my dealer was close by I could walk home if I had to drop my car off for repairs. There was a Honda dealer near my house, so I was going to go buy a Honda. Logical? I never looked anywhere else. I walked down to the Honda dealer and there was a woman sitting out in front and she happened to be the saleswoman on duty that day. I thought, "I'd like to buy a car from a woman." Notice my logic here? For some of you, it may seem totally absurd. I figured that you can get a lemon no matter how you make the decision. After I had looked at all the different Hondas on the lot, nothing was grabbing me. But, remember, I was going to buy a car *that* day. Finally, we walked around the lot and there in the corner of the lot was this white, pretty-looking car. I walked over and sat inside. There were gadgets all over the place and up to that point, I had never had a car with gadgets before. Pretty car. I would feel nice in it.

To make a long story short, I bought that car. But, it wasn't a Honda. It was a white Grand Am. I didn't read the consumers' report. I didn't read anything. The car was wonderful, by the way—it served me very well and I eventually sold it to a good friend.

How do you arrive at a decision (e.g., buying a car)? Do you like to go and look at all the different makes and models and test drive them all, or do you want to gather the data and decide?

Part of what happened to me in that decision-making process is that I am very strongly on the side of perceiving . . . I look at possibilities, all the time. I evaluate all the connections, rather than make a decision. There are times when I almost force myself to make a decision, that it seems almost irrational. I am not strong in the decision-making process . . . I am much stronger in gathering data. So there are times when I make decisions by saying, "You are going to do this by Friday," because I have to. Someone who is a decision maker, a judger, wouldn't have to do that—decision making comes easily to them. I behaved like a very quick decision maker the day I bought the car . . . the saleswoman was amazed. No one had ever bought a car like that from her. I spent a lot of money right there on the spot. This was so out of character for me, because I know I don't like the finality of decision making. For me, its much more fun when I am exploring all the possibilities. There are other people who can't stand to explore possibilities. And by the way, they don't make better decisions necessarily, because they may not look at all the facts before they make a decision. My story illustrates practice with a less preferred function. I know that I am much better at gathering facts than making decisions. So I force myself to keep deadlines for decisions. If you'll notice, I also made the decision as a true feeling type—noting my values and the later effect on others. It's always better to use all four functions when making a decision, but if we're honest with ourselves, we will notice that we usually err on the side of our perceiving and judging preference.

It is important to emphasize that no type is better than the other type! We each have our strengths and our weaknesses. I know people who think that they have decided something, because they've heard two sentences about it. They are clearly judgers. Whether they are judging by thinking or feeling, they have made that judgment about what is most important to them. Then they can say, "I'm finished with that; lets move on." Perceivers are never finished. We are constantly looking at more data. Even if we've made a decision, it is open to change, isn't it?

It's a miracle that we communicate at all and that we don't drive each other crazy in this world. And we are only talking about four different combinations. If you are into probability theory you may have already observed that four things taken four at a time produces 16 different types.

According to Jung, and more precisely to Myers-Briggs, you're either an introvert, I, or an extrovert, E; a sensor, S, or an intuitor, N; a thinker, T, or a feeler, F; and a judger, J, or a perceiver, P. Those are the possibilities. With E and I, we are talking about your energy source. With S and N, we are looking at the way you take in information—either you take it in with details (concrete reality) or you take it in as abstract with all the possibilities. With F and T, we are looking at the way you make a judgment. Either it is based on cause and effect, or values and human interaction—what meaning it has for you. And finally we have what your lifestyle is. If your lifestyle is J, what we call settled, fixed, decided, and ordered—everything has to be in its place or in lists; or it is P, open, fluid, and let-it-happen as it comes. So you're a quick decision-making person versus a possibility probing person.

Introverts, to be in society at all, get practice at doing their opposite all the time because they have to be out there. To be out there, they have to make themselves more extroverted than they would prefer. But they get good at doing that, so it's harder to know what they are. The theory states that we prefer one or the other. That doesn't mean we can't behave the opposite way when we have to. What we are looking at is preference not ability.

Some of the types are more honored in corporate America than are others. It is more honored to be in your office and getting your work done (I). It is more honored to notice the details of the job at hand (S). It is more honored to be logical (T). And time management skills are of the essence to be anybody in a corporate culture (J). Up until recently, corporate presidents had almost all been in the ISTJ category or ESTJ. That is what corporate America has been about. Quality emphasis is changing that. We are noting the need for greater strategic planning and systems thinking (N stuff!) as well as an emphasis on values, principles and the empowerment of people (clearly, F). We are seeing greater shifts in leadership styles and other types are climbing the corporate ladder.

One of the things you can start doing to learn and notice type is listen to people's words. You'll know someone is a sensor because you'll spot the frequent use of such phrases as: I want the facts; Let's look at the details; Let's get practical. An intuitor will say: Let's get to the point;

The theory as I see it is; So where is all of this leading us? The kinds of things that you'll hear from a thinker are brief, concise, to the point: It's clear; It's intuitively obvious; Don't take this personally. For a thinker, even emotions can be presented as if they are facts. Even when asked how they "feel" about something, the thinker will respond, "The fact is we need to consider this." So the way to communicate with a thinker is, "Let's look at the facts." Remember that those facts can be concrete details (S) or intuitive leaps (N)—they are still the facts! A feeler usually will be heard saying: How is everyone feeling about this?; Let's reconsider if this fits with our vision or our goals; Is this in everyone's best interest?

To communicate more effectively, you can respond differently to a person once you know how they prefer to operate and how they best can receive the message. Use the words that the person tends to use, "speak their language" to get your point across. You will want to be able to identify the types of the people you live with and work with, so that you can become like that type—at least momentarily while you are trying to communicate. It's all about rapport. Rapport is another way of giving recognition. It includes awareness and acknowledgment. It's about making a person feel that you understand who they are. So for someone who needs order, when you are giving directions, make sure some part of what you say includes step 1, step 2, etc. even if you are a person (N) who prefers to be given a general description of what is to be done so that you can work out the details. Always remember, everyone is not like you!

Rather than try to look at the way all 16 types want and can receive appreciation, I want to introduce the concept of temperament, which simplifies all types into four. Temperament theory goes far back to the ancient Greek division of sanguine, choleric, melancholic, and phlegmatic. A man named David Kiersey, in a book called *Please Understand Me* (Prometheus-Nemesis Press, 1984), discusses four temperament types based on the Myers-Briggs letters. You're either NF or NT, SJ or ST.

An NF is an intuitive, feeling person open to all kinds of possibilities around people. What an NF manager does best is help people recognize their strengths. The whole thrust of an NF is to facilitate people stroking, and most people respond well to this. NFs are usually extremely conscious about giving recognition. What they may be unconscious about is that their way of receiving it is not everyone else's preferred way.

In a team-building workshop at a branch of AT&T, one particular manager thought she was excelling with the way she acknowledged her employees. She would have a weekly meeting and call certain people up to the front so that they could tell everyone what they had done and receive the applause of their peers. This is something she had wished had been done for her for so long, and she was sure her staff was pleased. When I asked each person at our session to express how they wanted to receive recognition, no one in her group said they liked being singled out and brought to the front of the room. What she was doing to "recognize" them was actually embarrassing them! Her eyes were forced open. (And though at first she was startled, she became quite grateful.) "Pygmalian," "My Fair Lady," and "Pretty Woman" were all so popular because they carry the central theme—why aren't you all like me? I want so to make you over into an image of myself.

NFs want personal expressions of appreciation. It is important to them to be unique, so use the word "unique" in letting them know either about themselves or their contribution to the organization. Sure, there are a lot of people who *could* do the job, but there is no one who could do it exactly the same way. Be careful not to assume that NFs only want their feeling stroked. NFs also want to know that their feelings AND ideas are understood by others.

SJs need to know exactly what is going to happen and when. They do things within a given structure, and always on time. They give fine attention to detail and yet they do it within deadline. They appreciate being known as people who value thoroughness and accuracy. They are careful and cautious in what they do and they like that trait noticed. So, find ways of commending them for their loyalty, industriousness, and responsibility. Praise them for their product orientation. And if you are not the same temperament type, make note that they do want appreciation, but they probably will not show the pleasure in receiving it that your type might!

The NT is into knowledge for knowledge sake. There is a need "just to know" structured in their personality. They are mesmerized with the structures. An NT's best reward is his or her own excellent work. *Excellence* is the word you want to use with them if you want to give them a compliment. They do not want to be noticed for what they do routinely. Superior quality and competence are a given with an NT. Acknowledge their ideas—not just verbally— use them! Give them greater responsibility with a simple word about their capability. Stick with discussing reason and principle rather than personal qualities and above all else, listen to them.

The SPs are real artists. They are not usually professionals. They are so action-oriented that they don't usually ever make it to higher education. They like crises, and if there are no crises, they will create them. They are bright, but because so few people understand this common type they usually have had trouble in school. SPs have a lot of anxiety about being told what to do or how to do their work. They dislike anything that smells of "standard operating procedures." They want to be commended for their flair and grace. They are the people who have to be in there fixing, playing, doing, and trying it out and the way to recognize them is to let them be. Acknowledge with them that process is more important than product by not waiting until something is completed to give the reward. Take pride in their bravery, endurance, boldness, and cleverness. Let them know you appreciate their adaptability and sense of timing—especially if it is not the same as yours.

PUTTING IT TO WORK

By now, we are more aware of our own style and have probably had a few good insights into other's behavior that we may not have understood up until now. I hope so. The next thing we need to do is to put this information into practice. Analyze your company or department and see if you are treating everyone alike when it comes to recognition. It's simple to know what individuals want. Just ask them. And, be sure to ask them repeatedly, because even though some of our personality factors may not vary, we continue to change and our needs change accordingly.

One of the best ways to recognize employee differences is to take time out to attend a seminar or workshop that addresses them. You can use the Myers-Briggs, or some other tried and standard personality type system such as Enneagrams, or you can find companies and consultants who have created their own version. It doesn't really matter what system you decide to follow, as long as you use the results. Over 75% of the population are sensors, so using what you've just taught is essential to them. (And, I don't know of an intuitor who would balk at a theory working!)

There can be no packaged recognition program that works for everyone. Each organization will have to learn how to customize the needed training so that it meets the individual needs of its members.

So, now we have learned more about acknowledging people for their uniqueness. Even after you believe you've got the "individuality stuff" handled, your work is not complete. This business of recognizing individuals still leaves our organizations with a serious question, which has to do with our current team-building paradigm. How do you continue to recognize individuals while encouraging and fostering teams? Are we sending out mixed signals? We've placed a lot of emphasis on acknowledging the individual, now let's look at the team.

6

LEARNING TO CHEAT

One of the problems that exists in our companies today stems back to the educational system under which we were all raised. It's time we start teaching our children to cheat. Think about it. From our earliest experiences in the classroom, we are taught to "cover our papers" and be sure we are doing our own work. Students could be sent to detention or to the principal's office, or worse still, expelled if the teacher caught them cheating. Proctors watch students and some teachers give different tests to different rows so no one can possibly cheat. The penalties are severe. What message are we sending students when we tell them not to cheat? You must do it all alone. You have to be sufficient unto yourself. It is wrong to give or to receive help! What we are teaching is pure selfishness—an attitude that says, "What's mine is mine and never yours shall be." How can we expect these same children to grow up and work together in a spirit of teamwork and cooperation that is essential in business—and in life—today?

It doesn't seem to improve as we go higher up the academic ranks. As students reach the university level, they are often asked to sign or make pledges that they have not received help on a given assignment. I remember writing that oath on the bottom of my exams! We encourage students to work together and to study together right up to the exam, but when it comes to the final "reward" time, we tell them in no uncertain terms, "you are on your own now." It has tones of "the final judgment," a belief that says we come before God at the end of our lives and are asked to give an account. I'd rather believe that at the end of life I'll be "judged" on the measure of my love and co-operation, not on how well I worked out the answers alone! I'm convinced that belonging is one of our most basic needs.

We don't purposely intend to send mixed messages. And yet, even in places where things should be different, we often do. I teach in schools for adults where students are receiving bachelor degrees in business administration and even MBAs. According to the school's stated philosophy, we are encouraged to teach through participation and facilitation. We work in study groups that emulate real work groups. And yet many of the upper-level management teachers insist on giving closed-book, individual exams at the end of the semester! I have had various conversations with other faculty members on this point. For some people, you would think I was advocating anarchy! It's a challenging issue—how to balance individual learning and group performance. What does it mean to get a grade? What we believe about grades often carries over to the way we give rewards—A's to the winners, whatever that means.

I once gave a group exam and asked the students to use each other and whatever other materials they needed to answer the questions. It was interesting to note that they only felt free to work together with the people seated immediately near them. They stayed within their small defined study groups and never ventured to ask others in the room for help and no one thought—or dared—to come to me. They were never taught to ask for help from someone who might know—and so they never dreamed of doing that now! Once they had begun to relish the idea of working within their small groups, and became comfortable doing the exam collaboratively, they still weren't comfortable getting group grades. I had several students ask me to lower their grades because they thought they had gotten too much help from the group! How can we reprogram the message that says it is not okay to work together? How can we expect all the consultants in the world, and all the training exercises to teach people to work as teams? We need to change our messages. To teach teamwork and cooperation, we need to reassess something that is at the core of our culture—the spirit of competition.

The only time we teach children to work together is in team games when the spirit of competition is thick. Go out there and beat the other team. We are better. We can show them. Cheering squads are formed to yell, "Squash and kill the opponent." The other team becomes the enemy. And then parents send counter-messages that say, cooperate, share, and play fair. It's no wonder children are confused. And no wonder we remain confused as adults in the workplace when we are asked to work in teams and get rewarded for our individual performance.

Think of the game of musical chairs. It's a game that every child has played and I'm not sure too many like. Have you ever watched children play this game? First of all, there can only be one winner. Which, in effect, means that everyone else loses. If a child isn't quick enough, or competitive enough, or aggressive enough to grab a chair when the music stops, he or she is out of the game! One sad face after another exits in this sense of defeat until the one who can claim the greatest selfishness emerges triumphant.

Recently, I heard of a newer version of this game where the only way anyone could win was for everyone to win. The chairs continue to be removed one by one as the music stops, but the object of the game is for the children to fit as many as possible on the chairs remaining. This way, they have to figure out ways to cooperate rather than compete. Isn't this a better model?

Many of our companies are still working with the first version of musical chairs while saying they are using the second. "Our boss sends schizophrenic messages," one member of a finance team that I was working with told me recently. "He asks us to cooperate and work in cross-functional teams with people in other divisions, but then he puts up charts pitting one division against the other, judges us by 'the bottom line' and in meeting after meeting praises only the 'winners.'" How do you work together knowing this is the end result?

I once worked for a major communications company and had the opportunity to spend 30 days in intensive training—we affectionately termed the experience programmer's bootcamp. We were all put in a large room and were given progressively more difficult assignments as we learned the intricacies of coding and debugging mainframe software. After each module that we studied, we had to go to our supervisor's office and take an exam. If we got less than 100% on the exam, we were fired on the spot. No joke. After leaving all kinds of other jobs, and in many cases moving families, and households, the company fired you if you didn't EXCEL! The tension was incredibly high during that time and we became lifetime friends after having jointly endured that experience. But, the amazing thing was that while we had an enormous amount of talented individuals with varying abilities to study and cram for exams, or to do the actual programming for that matter, we were forbidden to speak to each other or give each other any help on the programs we were producing. Periodically, our supervisor came into the room to be sure we were sitting in this electric silence. I'm not sure how we survived. In fact, my group was the first to make it through the 30 days without losing anyone along the way. Psychologists would probably have a great time studying this phenomena. We were forced to be in a social setting where we should have been experiencing interdependence and community support, and yet were made to be separate and independent. The stress was great as it is in so many organizations that foster competition and alienation rather than building cultures of support and cooperation. The situation I have described is unfortunately not exaggerated.

The story gets more bizarre when you follow us into the workplace. Here, we were promptly told that successful programmers share information. Most programs are copied from other programs and minor changes are made to fit the new circumstances. We were told to ask questions and not to try to reinvent the wheel. We were put into groups and told to work as a team. How was this learning to take place? We were to undo everything we had fought so dearly to earn during the last 30 days. Weren't we getting mixed messages?

When we think of a normal work day, the 80-20 rule applies. At least for those who work in an office, most of their time is spent in meetings, or on the phone, or somehow collaborating with others. Very little of a manager's work life seems to be spent alone. In the study of personality theory, we discovered that almost 75% of the population are extroverts. That means that they have to hear what they are saying to even know what they are thinking. This obviously demands the cooperation of a listener. And for centuries, we have heard the expression, "two heads are better than one." We need to start to act as though we believe that is true—all of the time. We must start to look at the structures of our companies and of our award systems to see if we are creating a similar conflicting message to the one we've been given about cheating in school.

If we take a systems approach to companies, we will begin to reevaluate the way they are organized to see if they foster the concept of teams. One area that this is especially prevalent is in the way we give out awards and bonuses. Sometimes the very system that we create to give awards is the hindrance to creating the outcome we desire.

Consider the case of one consulting/systems engineering company. This company has excellent health insurance, retirement benefits, flexible hours, merit pay, and bonus systems. The employees are virtually assured of job security. Their bonus program looks great on the books. But, when it is examined, one notices that the way it is run causes decreased productivity rather than greater from middle manager on down. The amount of bonus money the company gives out varies from year to year because the total amount available for distribution is based on the company's total profits. The employees and management that are involved in the most profitable programs are the ones who receive the bonuses. Although this appears to be equitable, the company reorganizes frequently, which makes the bonus program very political. The manager who landed a multimillion dollar contract this year, when there was not much bonus money to distribute, may not be working this contract next year when the profit of his/her efforts are realized. Thus, the person most responsible for the profit may be left out of the bonus distribution. The way this bonus program is set up doesn't encourage middle management to strive for higher productivity or to search for new contracts. It motivates them to stay with contracts they have won and spend time protecting their "kingdom," instead of sharing information and contacts with others in an effort to acquire new contracts for the company. This recognition in the form of bonus, rather than being motivational, encourages territorialism and non-cooperation within and between divisions.

A New Jersey manufacturing company decided to pay its buyers bonuses if they kept the cost of purchases down. To make that happen, they were relying on second-tier sources and accepting poor-quality materials. The company was in the middle of a very big order, and the fasteners were lousy and ended up costing millions of dollars, while the sourcing department walked away with big bonuses.

In contrast, a participant at a Blanchard seminar uses his "Catch Me Doing Something Right" buttons to boost team spirit. Each person starts out with one button. When an employee sees a coworker doing something right, that employee could take the other's button. The only way the coworker could get another one was to spread the praise to someone else and take his/her button. Peer praising works to eliminate rivalries and jealousies that often are engendered in an office environment.

A Census Bureau fired 200 people recently rather than allow employees to take proportional work days as they had wanted. Management seemed terrified to having the workers cooperate in a crisis and resorted to the in-charge mode of firing. Need I mention the suffering morale of those remaining? Cases of burnout abound, not because of too much work, but because of the expectancy that our work is to be done in isolation. It is rooted in a belief that we are not members one of another. In the end, we are alone. Work together—but only when I tell you, and in the way that I find suitable. But when push comes to shove, you're all out there alone—it's your individual job that's on the line. Is this what we have come to in our competitive world?

I firmly believe that most of us want to work in atmospheres where community support and genuine compassion for each other is the rule rather than the exception. We have gotten off the track. We tend to separate the real us—the life we have outside the office from that which we are when we are at work. It requires a moment of pause and reflection and some old-fashioned remembering of time honored words like "Love one another" or the golden rule "Do unto others as you would have them do unto you." I've been fortunate to have never met anyone who basically disagreed with these principles. It's time we put them into practice.

We can learn a great deal about working in teams from the Japanese. Managers in the US are trained for specific, individual responsibilities. In Japan, the emphasis is on teamwork. American managers can threaten dismissal, while in Japan, executives take blame for mistakes and workers are guaranteed job security. Traditionally, the Japanese are steeped in the values of Zen Buddhism. Diligence, self-denial, and loyalty; these are among the qualities that make Japanese workers so productive.

In a study done by Personnel Psychology, 100 Japanese (27 to 57 years old) managers and a sample of American (29 to 52 years old) business managers were administered the Rokeach Value Survey and the Sarnoff Survey of Attitudes Toward Life, which measures desire for upward mobility. Results show that the Japanese attached greater importance to socially beneficial values, in contrast to the American emphasis on individuality and straight-forwardness. Yet, the Japanese also showed greater valuation of accomplishments and on the motivational instrument, more interest in advancement, money, and forward competition. It has been suggested in this study that achievement and advancement motivation may be important for Japanese productivity and that collective actions may be their only method for disciplining and rewarding it.

There is a tendency in Japanese organizations away from individual reward and recognition to recognition only for the group or organization. There is a high emphasis on security needs satisfaction, as well as social need for belonging. Personal relationships score high. They place a high value on training and education, especially of their young. Japanese companies are increasingly giving a percentage of profits to promote education, social welfare, and culture.

One place in America where we do learn to work as and reward teams is in sports. Jimmy Johnson, coach of the Dallas Cowboys, once said, "When you have success, there is glory for all. With success and glory come great feeling for one another and recognition of one another's contributions. If you keep harping on that time and time again with the players and have the credibility to back you up, you can somewhat prevent the 'star system.' You're not just throwing the word 'team' around loosely. The term is real and deeply felt. You have a team." This applies equally well in business.

There is a police captain in Walnut Creek, CA who developed a technique that reinforces the team concept. When someone goes out of his or her way to help another on the force, he or she receive a "champion card." This little device promotes such teamwork that several other city departments now use the cards as well.

Tennant, a company in Minneapolis that manufactures cleaning equipment, has peer recognition as part of each individual's performance review. The company takes recognition so seriously that it has become a true part of its corporate culture. In fact, Roger L. Hale, the company president, has coauthored a book, *Recognition Redefined* (Tennant Company, 1992), with Rita F. Maehling on how they have built employee self-esteem over the years by working on a company wide system. It's worth reading.

Organizations must recognize the spirit of collective groups as well as the spirit of an individual. All of this relates to understanding how to maintain the autonomy of individuals (they are authors of their decisions) and the spiritual nature of the human being (individuals must have meaning and relevance in life), which comes from creativity, social relationships, and production for the common good. Thus, there are multiple levels of recognition that need to be considered. We can all learn to be leaders by getting insight into the multiple dimensions of recognition of individuals and groups.

A case in point: John Sculley, former chairman and CEO of Apple Computer. *Fortune* magazine (July 26, 1993) noted, "Sculley likes to think of himself as Renaissance man, motivated by the thirst for knowledge rather than by ambition . . . Sculley's decision to step aside—in the middle of his five-year plan, just when products he nurtured are about to come to market—reflects not just trouble in Cupertino . . . It hints at a restlessness shared by a whole generation of talented business people." We are entering a Renaissance; an age of creativity; and an age of spiritual awakening. The baby-boomer workforce, now reaching mid-life, are seeking meaning and relevance from their work. There is a need to restructure reward systems in the workplace. One challenge of business today is to recognize this and create ways to reward it. In today's world, we long to work with a company or enterprise that has a higher mission and purpose (beyond profit); a mission in which workers can collectively believe and be made to feel a part of. Each of us wants to be acknowledged for our values, our beliefs, and our concerns for the common good. What greater recognition can one have.

Recognition is so much more than rewards and incentives. Currently, we give the latter primarily to individuals. What we need to do is to incorporate skills and techniques for peer recognition into every team-building training and team meeting. We can teach teams to honor individuals and celebrate and recognize the uniqueness that makes up that team. Perhaps, we need to give quality recognition to individuals and rewards to teams. Is that what's being done today in your organization?

7

RECOGNITION—BEYOND THE BONUS SYSTEM

If you were asked how you recognized employees in your organization (before you read this book), you might have responded the way most people do when they think of recognition. Companies today lump together anything they do for employees as recognition. These include profit sharing, stock options, bonuses, commissions, time off, plaques, trophies, certificates, contest, education, responsibility, suggestion boxes, point system contests, merchandise, food, fun, and cash. The list could go on almost endlessly. Yet, every child knows that "getting things" from mom and dad is not the same as feeling as if you matter and are appreciated. Psychologists have studied this for years. Psychiatrists and therapists of all types are hearing these cries on their couches and in their seminars. But there is little evidence that organizations have realized that this is the same thing they do when they give rewards to employees.

For true quality recognition to be taking place, both groups and individuals must feel that they make a difference, that what they think and say is important to the organization and that the extra effort they put into their work really matters. I acknowledge that this is a lofty goal, but I remember a saying that "it is better to aim high and miss the mark than to aim low and make it!" If total quality is ever to really change the way our corporations think and act, organizations have to start somewhere. Many start with training programs, some focus on SPC, and others on team building. Gurus argue that the commitment and implementation must come from the top. Does that mean that every employee in a company whose CEO is not behind the quality bandwagon should throw up his or her arms and quit? That's the impression you get when you read a lot of the quality literature. I hardly believe that is true. Systemic change can take place by revolution or evolution and evolution often starts in some small, often obscure way.

Although what I advocate is nothing short of a revolution on the way we view and appreciate employees, an evolutionary approach is not discounted. We've got to start somewhere. In the case of recognition, although an all-out change in culture is needed and desirable, some change—even some token program—can be better than nothing. Most adults have come to realize that their parents "meant well" when they received "toys instead of love" and all would probably admit that this was better than not receiving anything at all.

This is the way I view what companies are doing today to "reward" employees. There can be a chasm existing between dispensing rewards and truly recognizing employees. I'm not asserting that this is always the case, but I am suggesting that we give this some serious thought. In the meantime, once you've mastered (or at least begun to look at!) the awareness stage of recognition, you can go on to appreciation and acknowledgment. Although I have emphasized that this should be a regular occurrence, I'm not advocating that we do away with all the programs that are already in place to show appreciation. What I am suggesting, however, is that we take a serious look at whether or not they are accomplishing the goal of true quality recognition or if they have become a way of being smug in believing that "sure, we recognize our members/employees. Look at the programs we run."

Some companies may need to do away with all the reward programs that currently exist until they develop a sincere recognition culture. Too many programs exist, just so the company can pay lip service to having actually read the 14 points! If you ask the employee, he or she might tell you that the program not only doesn't do what it was intended too, but, perhaps, even has the opposite effect in some cases.

But be careful not to too easily throw out the baby with the bath water. Programs and rewards are not necessarily bad. In fact, some are actually achieving the end for which they were created. You simply need to find out which category your organization is in.

To help you analyze your own program, this chapter will raise some questions and give you ideas. By looking at some programs in place—samples of what companies are already doing—you'll more objectively be able to analyze what works and what doesn't so you can start off with a clear understanding.

In addition to describing the sample programs, in some cases, where I have had direct involvement or have at least been able to ask, I've endeavored to show how employees feel about them as well. Perhaps you'll find yourself or your organization here. In all cases, I'll raise the questions that we need to be asking ourselves if we truly want *Recognition: The Quality Way.* Try to be objective—especially if you've spent years, money, and a lot of committee meetings developing a program you thought was great!

The following examples are by no means exhaustive and don't pretend to be conclusive research. There have been too many written exposés of the best and most excellent companies, who by the time the books have gone to press, have fallen off the top 10 list and in some cases, even fallen off the charts of existence. So instead, I decided to simply get an eclectic feel for what is out there. Many companies continue to pollinate and create from within, never knowing what else is available. And many companies, like their management philosophies, believe that what they are doing about recognition is "just fine" and that their employees are quite satisfied with their efforts. Looking at other companies might be a less threatening way of analyzing your own efforts.

Benchmarking techniques have taught us to look outside ourselves to see what is working. I, along with several colleagues and students, interviewed companies across America to get the following information. We started with a very random sample and got some discouraging results. We heard about a lot of ways that "it wasn't working" or about "mediocrity." These will serve as useful for our self-reflection as well.

We then used suggestions from associations and affiliations that we already had, as well as programs that we had heard about in the press so that we could find out what other people were pleased with. The samples here then are meant to be representative, not all inclusive, and not even "the best." If you do decide you want to give out rewards, think of this chapter as a brainstorming session of ideas that you can use to start the process of generating more of your own. Remember that uniqueness is key. If you are looking for more suggestions on how to "give rewards," read *1001 Ways to Reward Employees* (Workman, 1994) by Bob Nelson, a management specialist and vice-president of New Product Development at Blanchard Training and Development. I do, however, suggest you read what others are doing with a critical eye and find out if employees truly experience the recognition the company says it gives.

While reading, be sure to also consider the other chapters of this book and some of the other ideas presented here to ask if your "programs" really are quality recognition. For example, do they support individuals while exalting teams? Do they take into account uniqueness? Do people feel that they are being used and then thanked, or that they really matter and make a significant difference in the life and working of the company?

You might be curious about the initial survey. I'll first present those results. When we started this research, we developed a questionnaire that was answered by over 100 companies. Most of the surveys were filled out by someone in human resources—most frequently the manager. We purposely did not use any companies known for their "excellent programs." The results are summarized here:

RECOGNITION SURVEY

1. What was the driving force behind developing your organization's recognition program?

   A. to increase employee morale (32)
   B. to enhance employee ownership towards corporate values, standards and company/mission (25)
   C. to excelerate "employee peak performance" (21)
   D. to complement existing career development programs (9)
   E. to reduce employee turnover (15)
   F. to increase the standards of newly hired personnel (9)

To truly evaluate a recognition program, we first have to consider why it was originally formed. Although companies did talk about surveying their employees, none of the companies we interviewed were using statistical measures to find out what effect their programs were really having.

2. What form(s) does your recognition program take?

    A. merit raises (16)
    B. bonuses (24)
    C. individual incentive plans (25)
    D. group incentive plans (7)
    E. merchandise/recognition incentives (19)
    F. contests/material rewards (14)

This list shows a real misunderstanding of some of the motivational theories. Bonuses, incentives, and raises are considered as recognition more frequently than anything else. Do people really feel "seen, heard, and understood" when they receive a bonus? Incentives and rewards are not the same as recognition! We noticed that most companies lump everything a company does for an employee as recognition. It's a common pitfall.

3. If your program offers a form of "money" as an incentive, what is your organization's rationale because we know that studies show that money isn't the No. 1 motivator in changing performance over long periods of time?

Among all the managers surveyed, there appeared to be a common misconception that money is the No. 1 motivator. A few companies acknowledged that it was only a short-term motivator and therefore suggested that merchandise, time off, and personal recognition were really the main motivators. Employee after employee, however, said they weren't really working for the money. They wanted the respect and feeling that who they are and what they did made a difference.

4. To what extent does your recognition program increase: productivity? morale? profits? How do you measure this?

About ⅓ of the companies could not give any meaningful answer to this question. We got a lot of "I don't knows." Others said they measured these things by how many people received quarterly recognition, how many meetings were held, what teams had actually accomplished (e.g., sales results and production goals against actuals). From the rest, we got some really vague answers like, "We don't measure, but we know that when morale is up, production is up, and profits do increase."

5. How long has your program been in effect?

The answered varied from company to company, anywhere from two months to 100 years!

6. How frequently do you modify/enhance this program?

Most responses were "not very often." There was no certain frequency. Only a handful of companies responded yearly. Two companies said as needed, or in an ongoing way. It is obvious that the idea of continuous process improvement needs work when it comes to the area of recognizing employees!

7. How was the program developed and who was involved in the process?

About one-half the respondents said that the employees helped to set up the programs with input and approval from the executive boards. The rest said it was simply set up by human resources or dictated by the government!

Only one company had used an outside consultant. (I purposely did not use any companies I had consultant with so as not to bias the study.)

8. How does your program enable employees to make suggestions regarding the type of recognition that will be the best motivator, and how effective do you believe this process is?

Almost all the companies who responded to this question (can we assume that the rest don't ask their employees?) had a suggestion box of some sort and the effectiveness varied widely.

Here are some poignant comments we received:

"What good is the suggestion box when no one ever answers my requests? They don't let us know if they read them and they certainly don't ever seem to do anything we suggest."

"Sure they read these things, and the CEO (or more likely his secretary), sends out a form letter saying thank you for the suggestion, but then that's the last we ever hear of it."

"Suggestion boxes are good for improving processes, why do they confuse this with recognizing employees?"

9. What have you found to be the most effective and most popular long-term motivator in your recognition program?

Every respondent said that direct acknowledgment of the employee was the most effective over the long run. (It's amazing that although they all knew this intuitively, almost no one knew how to do it effectively.) Also, job stability and satisfaction are effective when they can be promised. Training, raises, and promotions were listed more than once. Again, the confusion exists between job-security and pay issues and recognition.

10. For the most part, do you believe that companies, in general, take into consideration the type of em-

ployee they are trying to motivate prior to deciding on the vehicle to use as motivation?

Generally, the response was no. Most companies give blanket types of rewards without any consideration of the individual person who will be receiving the reward. No one ever asked the employee if the reward was meaningful, as the following responses attest:

"Cups, caps, keyrings. . . . These do more to get the company some free advertising than they do to give me a pat on the back. If they really cared, they'd give me something that was meaningful to me—however small it is."

"I don't feel recognized when almost everyone gets the same reward in spite of the obviously outstanding work done by some."

One company has different programs of recognition according to the different level of the employee. (What the employees said in these cases is unprintable!)

11. Does your program promote teamwork or competition between employees? Explain.

There was an equal response between teamwork and competition. One company responded, "Yes, we have jobs that are accomplished by various levels. We use cross-functional teams." And, they felt that being invited to be part of a cross-functional team was recognition enough.

On the positive side, we had several companies that began to look at how much competition they were actually promoting and as a result of this survey promised to consider rewarding teams!

12. Do your managers, for the most part, support the recognition program?

Fortunately, the majority of respondents said that their managers do support the programs. Thirteen companies refused to respond on the grounds that their answers might incriminate them! And one company actually said no because there was too much paperwork involved!

13. What type of role do your managers play in the recognition program?

In many of the companies, the managers played a major role in evaluating who would get the reward. Some managers served as reward presenters. Only one company talked of peer recognition; the rest underlined that it was the managers responsibility for recognizing deserving employees and for establishing the process for prompt reviews.

In a few cases where employees were more involved in peer recognition, the managers did say that they felt responsible for encouraging employees to participate in the award programs. They felt personally responsible for morale building and believed they should be the key supporters and the driving force behind any programs. Lower-level managers thought they needed to represent employees to upper management.

14. Is your CEO supportive of, and active in, your recognition program?

All of the companies we interviewed said their CEOs were supportive but not involved, except perhaps in a one-time award ceremony at which they presided. (What kind of message does this portray about the importance of these programs?)

15. How is your recognition program communicated to new and current employees?

We got answers of word of mouth from other employees, employee assistance programs, employee manuals, memos, newsletters, bulletin boards, voice mail, quarterly meetings, supervisors, new employee orientation, and "all of the above."

16. Have you surveyed your employees on their feelings of your recognition program?

Most companies said that they did survey their employees anywhere from every three months to every three years, but few companies had really made any changes in their existing programs as a result.

It is far better not to ask employees for their input if that input is not going to be used immediately.

17. How did your employees rate the program overall?

Most responses ranged from good to fair with a few saying that the programs made absolutely no difference.

18. What type of career development program do you offer within your organization to help employees participate in reaching their performance goals and proceeding to the next level of responsibility/assignment?

The larger companies cited their training curriculums and tuition reimbursement programs. None of the companies had a plan in place to be certain that every individual employee was meeting his or her career objectives.

What they cited were internal job posting systems, training courses that could be used for advancement, some exposure to such courses as "Managing personal growth," and other management development programs. Many companies had mandatory training hours per year but no real guarantee of career enhancement as a result. A few companies were partnering with local universities to offer college-level or extension courses for advancement.

One company told us about a management rotation program where managers could learn about other positions within the company. Others cited the learning that comes from working on a team or focus group.

19. Are your managers and supervisors provided with training that reinforces and complements effective performance?

Most responded yes and in two cases, coaching and leadership training were cited as well as continuing education on motivation and management with a strong emphasis on people as our most essential resource.

20. Do you believe that your employees feel as though "someone in the organization really knows who they are?"

One group said yes for most of their management and supervisory levels but no for those at lower levels of support. A few companies mentioned temporary staff and said they thought they were perceived as "just a body doing a job."

Several simply answered, "We try to give positive feedback and encouragement" or "We do care about our people." (I'm not so certain anyone really even understood the question!!)

21. What does your company spend per employee (per year), to operate your recognition programs?

One company responded $10,000 per year—but on further questioning, we found they were referring to health benefits!

Four companies quoted 2–5% of the person's salary, while the rest had no idea!

22. What advice would you like to give about developing recognition programs?

The following responses indicate how the participants felt:

"Fear can only get a body to work. You have to be more creative to inspire your employees."

"Reward and recognition programs are a necessity for competitive companies."

"Be sure to tie recognition to the company mission, vision, and values."

"Make sure you reward both team and individual accomplishments"

"Only award teams, not individuals."

"Survey employees to see what they want."

"Tie your program to business goals and objectives. The link between the two is what makes it work."

"Avoid favoritism."

"Plan incentives that would be attractive to all age groups."

"It's important to help people develop their confidence and self-worth because when this happens, the other people will follow."

"Only recognize outstanding service and performance."

"Be sure to provide attainable goals, specific criteria, and consistency in application."

"Encourage high visibility of the program."

"There must be commitment from up top for the program to succeed."

"Provide choices."

Some Stories and Comments from Our Interviews:

"My basic philosophy in life has been, recognize me for what I can do, not what I say I can do. I have supported this with a strong propensity for telling the truth. This truth aspect has lead to a few problems when I tell it like it is but watch others rise because they told the boss what he wanted to hear. I wonder if the managers really know who is doing the work they reward?"

"I don't believe that employee-of-the-month programs really provide any improved morale or motivation. Typically the cheerful, responsible, highly motivated individuals who are selected would be cheerful, responsible, and highly motivated without the program. These programs do nothing for the vast majority of workers who, all things being equal will NEVER be employee of the month. Similar to a corporate CEO getting another performance bonus, while the guy on the assembly line gets nothing, a program such as this increases the distance between the 'haves' and the 'have nots,' so that the employee of the month has probably already been highly recognized."

"I appreciate the respect I receive for a job well done. That does not necessarily equate to more money, but it feels good to have someone request my presence on a team or as part of an effort."

"In May, I received an award for managing the construction of a new building and associated parking garage. We have just received our yearly performance review, and I was chided for not putting the fact that I received the award in my part of the review. I had forgotten it, and it is hanging on my wall near my desk. So you can see that it did not have any lasting effect. In fact, I was embarrassed to get it. I was in charge of a team who worked on the project. I did put many long hours in, and was the driving force within the team, but I was embarrassed that no one else was mentioned. Also my name was spelled wrong on the award. A sure way to motivate someone!"

"In addition to a recent program that was started at Health & Hospitals, we have gotten occasional 'attaboy's.' In fact, the year before last, my boss gave me and a couple of members of my group a short memo congratulating us on a job 'well done' (we had just finished project managing the installation of two of the largest telephone systems in New York City during the prior three years).
The memo appears to be a nice touch; unfortunately, one memo (good for the file) does not erase the bad taste we get in our mouths every week, when his behavior clearly indicates his concerns that we don't seem to know what we're doing."

"Company parties are nice, but it really does something for me when my manager goes to the trouble to write a personal note of appreciation for something I've done."

"When merit raises must average x% per department, there is a tendency for some very talented individuals to get penalized just because they work with an exceptionally good group of people. Something's very wrong here."

"We found that by ASKING our employees, rather than TELLING them what was needed to solve our problems, our solutions were much more effective. We need to find ways to do more of this."

"The fulfillment of the basic human need of being recognized is a great motivating factor for employees. I use this fact to keep employees striving for success even in otherwise difficult circumstances. I use verbal and written recognition. The verbal recognition can be over a cup of coffee, a pat on the back, or public mention during staff meetings. The written communication comes in the form of a personal note from me, accompanied by a frameable certificate and a $50 check. I call this an on-the-spot award and I give them out without warning."

"This type of communication is great for internal recognitions, but it is not the most important recognition mechanism. The most important recognition is external. We are a service company, so when a customer commends an employee I make a big to-do about it. The employee will get a 'customer initiated award,' which includes a $50 award, certificate, and a letter from me and the customer. I've always found it interesting that in our internal awards the $50 check is the most 'looked-forward to' recognition. But in the external award, the letter from the customer carries the most weight."

"It is probably time to take a look at the military's award system. The soldiers of today's army are very different than they have ever been in the past. Approximately 96% of the soldiers entering the service today are high school graduates, and many of them even have bachelor's degrees. Their personal goals and the ways they are motivated are much different than the 'old army.' It is a good system, but it could use a little renovation."

"Communication as a method for responding to basic human needs . . . to be seen, heard, and understood, has become a priority within my organization. Until recently, much of the internal communication in my organization was unresponsive to its intended audience. Management told employees what the employees should think and feel, and how they should act. Employees responded by ignoring management communication. They felt neglected, and ignored.
Within the last two years, my company has revised its methods of communication to emphasize employee recognition, encourage employee input and acknowledge employees contributions to the success of the company. A good example of how these positive changes were enacted is our organization's President's Quality Awards. Employees can be nominated by customers, peers, or their managers. All nominees receive a letter of recognition and plaque from the company president, a recognition luncheon, and recognition prizes. Those em-

ployees that are selected as finalists for team contributions, and/or individual accomplishments receive substantial cash awards, and a national recognition awards program at our headquarters in Dallas, *TX*."

"Employees have been encouraged to express their opinions and submit their ideas to management on ways to improve the business through a formal idea submission program, and open access to executive management through the company newsletter and 800-number comment lines. The results of these changes has been a dramatic improvement of employee morale, productivity, and loyalty to the organization. Certainly it can now be said that my organization has handled its communication problems very well. The basic human needs of my organization's employees are now being addressed. Every employee has the opportunity to be 'seen, heard, and understood.' The need to . . . 'be listened to, to feel recognized, acknowledged, appreciated, and accepted,' is no longer being ignored. There are good things ahead for everyone within my organization because of these significant changes."

"I was pleased with the amount of feedback I received on my goal of informal acceptance at work. While writing that report, it made me examine my personal beliefs about acceptance at work. Was I trying to get awards or be part of the team? I have received awards and cash ($550) for working as a team player. In retrospect, to be sought out to contribute to the team meant more to me than awards or cash. I will display the awards and spend the cash. However, if I can't get along with my coworkers, then I will leave."

"Senior management should conduct an impact analysis and identify the people who will be adversely affected by the implementation of the new system. Special change management programs, such as office refurbishment, new business planning, and retraining should be conducted to prepare the current staff for the takeover of the new system. A contribution award scheme should be set up as an incentive to encourage the current staff to contribute ideas towards the design of the new system, despite the fact that some current staff will still need to be replaced."

EXAMPLE WHERE A WHOLE
PROGRAM BACKFIRED

At a large supermarket chain in southern California, the employee recognition program includes a yearly nomination for a King and Queen of Courtesy, a courtesy Clerk of the Year, and a Cashier of the Year. Once a year, each store sends in ballots for their individual store winners who then compete on a district-wide basis. District winners then compete on a chain-wide basis.

It is unclear what the criteria is for winning at the local store level. The protocol for the process of getting employees on a winning ballot is up to each individual store director, and as a result its application varies greatly from store to store. Some stores have instituted an Employee-of-the-Month contest leading up to the yearly competition, while others simply choose a winner based on a decision by the store director and a manager. Some have all employees vote.

In addition, this recognition program excludes front-line management from participating, as it was originally structured for nonexempt employees. There are no recognition programs either chain-wide or on an individual store basis to reward outstanding operational performance by line management.

EXAMPLES OF REWARD SYSTEMS,
PROGRAMS, AND EVENTS

Evart Products Co., an automotive parts supplier to Chrysler, has a Quest Plan that provides a bonus when the company performance improves. For instance, if a 5% bonus is earned by the company for performance improvements, each employee receives an additional 5% of his or her wages as a bonus. Gainsharing, along with an employee suggestion program, helped Evart to reduce its defect rate from 437 parts per 10,000 down to 2 parts per 10,000. They feel that their Quest Plan has accomplished its goal of high employee involvement and improved motivation, which clearly improved productivity. Success did not come overnight. Evart implemented the Quest Plan in 1987 and in 1991 was finally able to claim the outstanding defective parts rate they still hold today.

At **Starbucks Coffee Co.,** employees are offered an innovative employee ownership plan through Bean Stock, a stock option program. Starbucks is exceptionally unique in that any employee who has been employed from April 1st to the end of the fiscal year in September, and who works more than 20 hours, is eligible for stock. If still employed in January, eligible employees receive awards based on annual salaries. The company goal has been to provide options equal to 10% of each employee salary. The program was begun by President and CEO Howard Schultz, whose belief is that success and profits should touch each and every eligible employee, not just the few at the top. Schultz says, "Everybody will have a stake in financial rewards. We're all equal." Evart employee involvement coordinator Jim Walker, suggests that, "There has to be an attitude that you're in this for the long term, that it's going to work." Employee ownership supports this philosophy.

Wal-mart believes that everyone should share the profits. Almost all Wal-mart workers are stockholders through the company's ownership plan. Some have become quite wealthy through it. Bonuses are earned based on the individual's store's profits rather than on competitive sales among workers. Although this is not really recognition, it seems to foster more of a team spirit that separates this Arkansas based retailer from other discounters.

Southwest Airlines has the fewest customer complaints in the industry. Their officers work at least once every quarter among the ranks. They serve as baggage handlers, ticket agents, or flight attendants and get to see first-hand what the other employees deal with on a day-to-day basis. The other employees love it.

In a column Ken Blanchard wrote for *Success* magazine, he tells about a man named Drew Diamond, a regional manager for **Holiday Inns** in Tennessee. Diamond found a way to monitor the service guests received when the hotel manager wasn't around. He had his manager give guests a book of coupons as they checked in. Whenever a guest felt they had received outstanding service, they were to fill out a coupon and give it to the manager who would then personally commend every employee noted. Within a few months, service in the hotel improved considerably.

Years ago, several airlines had instituted the same service. I made it a practice of asking for the names of those attendants who did something one step above and they were always delighted. One of them told me that she had amassed hundreds of dollars of free-dinner coupons from American Express as her reward. This, she confided in me, meant far more to her and her husband than the annual bonus.

Montgomery Ward has an "Associate-of-the-Month" program for someone who goes out of his or her way to give outstanding service. Winners receive a gift as well as a certificate and a gold name badge.

According to Dr. Gerald H. Graham, distinguished professor of management at the W. Frank Barton School of Business at The Wichita State University in Kansas, when he questioned over 100 Montgomery Ward managers at a workshop, he found that more than 90% of the people kept the ribbons, certificates, or plaques they had received for over 20 years. Some even cited stories of ribbons they had since elementary school.

Blue Cross/Blue Shield of Alabama recently increased the number of adjudicated claims by 300% in less than 30 months without changing the number of staff members. They attribute it to simple changes they made in their feedback system and increased employee reinforcement.

Fel-Pro, a gasket manufacturer, sends letters to all employees who make suggestions for improvement. At their annual Christmas party, there is a drawing from the letter file and several people win $1,000 awards. People also get prizes for the best suggestions of the year. Individuals have to believe they actually have a chance with hard work, and a little luck, of receiving an award.

Mary Kay Cosmetics is often recognized as one of the top 100 most motivating companies to work for. Because most of the employees are independent sales consultants, appreciation is mostly shown for superior sales. In the past, outstanding producers could receive such things as mink coats, diamond rings, first-class trips, a burgundy Pontiac Grand Am and of course, the famous pink Cadillac. Newer prizes continue to be added, because the company is now attracting a greater number of men to their sales force.

What is especially unique about these prize awards is that there is no limit to the number of people who can receive them. Each person is therefore only in competition with himself or herself.

According to a group of representatives, the annual awards ceremony is the "party of the year" and everyone strives to get invited to some of the "inner-circle" parties. The invitation itself is a coveted award. Even seating is based according to sales, so everyone strives literally, "to be up-front." Awards are given for sales as well as recruiting. It is one of the companies strongest beliefs that no one can get ahead without helping others.

In addition to sales awards, the company offers extensive training to their people at all levels. "We are recognized by being given opportunities to learn, to grow, and to gain focus. We know that we are more than a sales number. Each person in our organization is made to feel that his or her career is important to the company. Every effort is made to help you be successful."

Training ranges from annual and biannual seminars to individual video and audio cassette programs. There are weekly unit meetings and a one-on-one mentor program. There is constant feedback and encouragement, applause, and awards. In her book on people management, Mary Kay Ash says, "If you were to pin the whole book down to the most important point, I would say it's praising people to success."

The bumble bee pin has become a company symbol to remind these people that they can go beyond what they ever thought possible. "Aerodynamically, the bee can't carry it's own weight and shouldn't be able to fly. But, obviously, it does."

Praxair Inc., a semiconductor-process gasses facility in Kingman, AZ, has a special annual event: quality days. The celebration takes a full week where every person in the organization receives some special recognition. During one day in particular, management lessens workloads and encourages employees to participate in the ongoing program. This program includes quality-related videos as well as a luncheon in everybody's honor.

Insight Electronics, an entrepreneurial company in San Diego, CA, believes that the first recognition the employees need is to be paid well. It is really hard for an employ to take that extra step if they feel they could be getting more mney somewhere else. One of the first things the new president did two months after he took over was to give every employee a $100 cash bonus. He asked their human resources department to do some research on national pay averages for each job description and then proceeded to adjust all pay to the 90th percent of the national average.

The company also believes in employees getting as much education as time permits and they are given 50% tuition reimbursement for any college classes they attend. They have created something called Insight University where for two full working days, plus a weekend, everyone meets and networks with all 10 other divisions at a resort. They train by day and play by night. How are they able to afford this? "Our profits have almost doubled in the last two years. Our suppliers now pay for over 80% of the training because of the results."

At **Peninsula Bank,** tellers and new-account desk personnel have the opportunity to become "certified." There are a series of requirements, like product sales and referrals culminating in a monetary award, plus a plaque and desk award. The person who has been certified is also recognized at review time with a promotion or raise. The program has served as a positive reinforcement for others as well. Those who haven't yet been certified have the attitude, "If they can do it, so can I."

The manager of the special recognition program, Alex Reyes, describes **Bank of America's** philosophy this way: "The bank is strongly committed to recognition as a key part of our corporate values. Service awards have been given for many years. We have a strong program, but commitment to our company, particularly during the past five years or so, is genuinely appreciated."

He recently reviewed the company's service award program with 660 employees and found that employees wanted better gift choices, more items for business use (e.g., a leather portfolio case), as well as recognizable brand names and clearer distinctions among levels.

In the past, employees were sent a card prior to their service anniversary date and they selected gift and returned the card to the vendor without their manager's involvement. One finding the bank made was that the employees wanted the managers to be more involved. Now, managers receive notification of the service anniversary, and they inform the employee. This gives them a chance to personally thank the employee for service and to comment on specific parts of the employee's performance for which he or she deserved recognition. Bank of America's former CEO, A.W. Clausen, has spoken with managers about the importance of employee recognition, and a variety of written materials have been distributed to managers about their role in the process.

In a large computer supply company that prefers to go unnamed, the human resources department did a study recently as part of their exit interviews to find out why employees were leaving the company. They found that women were looking for more recognition and growth and the men were looking for stability, security, and salary. Women were also looking for a "balance" of work and personal life that their company didn't offer. Some left because of lack of ethics. But in 75% of the interviews, what really came through was that they were leaving because of lack of growth and recognition.

From a former defense contractor: "In our downsizing and restructuring environment, recognition primarily includes holding regularly scheduled employee meetings, focusing on the restructuring of the organization. We have an even stronger need now for ongoing communication. There is a bulletin board updated regularly on the computer network and it remains accessible for any employee who wishes to access current data. Keeping employees notified of any changes has become vitally important."

Pioneer Data Systems in Johnston, IA, had a program for employees who got MAD. Their reward program was based on "Making a Difference" and employees nominated themselves, a peer, or a workgroup. Their division looked for people who came up with a creative solution to end-user computing problems that saved the company time, and therefore money, or helped a user become more independent of their services.

The program was judged by a committee of one constant and three rotating members and awards were given out at monthly departmental meetings. The reward was a coupon redeemable for a half-day's vacation, usually taken the day before actual vacation time, to get a head start.

The program gradually faded away, but it created an atmosphere where people began to find reasons to praise one another directly. Exactly the point!

Buck Knives is a family-owned company that engenders long service through loyalty and a feeling of familiarity with the Buck family. The Buck vision statement includes "developing our people" as well as products and services to consistently surpass customer expectation. The first two of their mission statements speak of training, empowering, and rewarding employees for teamwork, creativity, and calculated risk-taking. The 400+ employees cherish the opportunity to openly meet in roundtable to interact with the leaders and do feel that their input is heard.

One of the most popular forms of recognition is "time off with pay"—up to three weeks per year as well as Friday afternoons. In an employee survey, 90% chose the time-off option over cash.

Los Angeles-based **Super Shuttle** gives their shuttle bus drivers paid days off when their performance exceeds their own typical rate!

The **Ziff Institute,** at the Computer Training and Support conference, gives an ASSIST award (a beautifully designed sculpture) to people or organizations who have contributed "above and beyond" to the computer training industry. During the previous year, companies or individuals can nominate themselves or others and a team of peers across the country select the winners. Those who have won it prize the recognition of their peers.

A few years ago, **Acura,** headquartered in Gardena, CA, also commissioned an artist to create a limited edition crystal sculpture for the best dealership. These one-of-a-kind pieces could not be bought anywhere else.

The **YMCA** in San Diego, CA, uses a system of peer recognition where each cluster nominates candidates for an award to be given at their bimonthly meeting. What is unique about them is that there is no selection process. Everyone nominated gets an award. The awards are divided into five categories:

1. The "Swiper" Award—for the individual who creatively used another's idea for the benefit of his/her own program.

2. The "Change Maker" Award—for someone who initiates and welcomes change, or constructive criticism for his or her own improvement.

3. The "Risk Taker" Award—for the person who took a risk and got up and tried again. This award rewards trying.

4. The "Miracle Ear" Award—for the one who listens to a peer, a member, or participant's suggestions and puts those suggestions into action.

5. The "Wild Blue Yonder" Award—for any individual who goes above and beyond the call of duty.

McDonnell-Douglas provides a substantial reimbursement for any educational course that any of its 112,000 employees wants to take—work related or not. CEO John F. McDonnell's rationale for continuing this program while cutting hundreds of millions of dollars elsewhere is simple, "A total quality management system is based on people, and people who are learning are more open to improvement, change, and risk-taking. This is the kind of person we need."

After several years of low earnings and high layoffs, **Goodyear Tire and Rubber** hired Stanley C. Gault who, within two weeks of his arrival, had personally spoken to more than 3,000 workers about their jobs. He solicited their ideas on how company performance could be improved. The "associates," as his employees are now called, were delighted with the change.

At a **McDonald's** franchise in Ramona, CA, there is a program known as TLC—both for Tender Loving Care and for Thinking Like a Customer. Employees receive McBucks for doing a number of things that their managers recognize as "extra." McBucks are color coded and expire monthly and there are two levels of prizes awarded at the manager's meetings. The lower level is given to anyone who has earned 100 or more and the upper level to those over 200. All McBucks from the TLC program go into a drawing box and a drawing for a weekend getaway for two takes place twice a year.

They also have a unique program to help develop crew members into management. Managers work side by side with a potential manager, who they call a buddy. When the crew person is promoted and passes their six-month manager review, the manager who worked side by side with the buddy receives a $100.00 bonus.

Tonkin, Inc. is a recognition materials supplier headquartered in Seattle, WA. Ironically, their employees never receive the plaques, jewelry, watches, luggage, and other goods that they manufacture. What they do have, however, is a weekly breakfast or lunch to honor all those who have met their objectives for the week and these meetings are attended by all company executives.

The company also has a once a month "family night" at a local pizza parlor or some other restaurant where individuals and teams are honored in the presence of their husbands, wives, and children. Their monthly company magazine also carries a family-oriented theme. In addition to corporate news, sections are included that record such things as births, graduations, and anniversaries. One of the employees favorite "benefits" is that 82% of all major positions are held by internally promoted employees.

Ben & Jerry's Ice Cream from Vermont also promotes from within whenever possible. All employees have the option to purchase stock at a 15% discount, not just top management. The base salary for the top executives cannot be more than seven times the lowest paid full-time employee. The company also provides low interest rates for employees to purchase a house.

Ben & Jerry's wants their employees to enjoy working. There is a unique in-house internship program, where an employee can be scheduled for on-the-job training for a position in the company that he or she thinks might be enjoyable. The internship gives both the employee and the company an opportunity to assess the fit.

A group of employees is assigned to the "Joy Gang" and their whole purpose is to find ways to recognize employees and bring them joy. A special company budget has been set aside for this purpose. There is also a "Graft Box," which has different gifts and surprises that the employee can choose from once they get enough "markers" for good deeds or outstanding performance.

Women get a six-week fully paid maternity leave with an additional six months at 60% of salary. Fathers also get paternity leave, up to 12 weeks with 2 weeks full pay. There is also an adoption plan where parents can get four weeks off with full pay as well as a $1500.00 gift to help pay the cost of adoption.

There is a week set aside each year especially to recognize employees. But, supervisors can give group or individual recognition at any time when daily, weekly, or monthly goals are met or surpassed. And of course, there is always the three free pints of ice cream every day!

SOME RESEARCH ON REWARDS

McCormick and Ilgen, authors of the text *Industrial Psychology* (Prentice-Hall, 1980), give us an interesting way to divide the common appreciation techniques used in most organizations today. Their system can be illustrated by a four-quadrant grid because most reward systems are based on presence (simply being a member of an organization), or performance and are either initiated by managers or by a company program (see Table 7.1).

In one study, a target population of 800 health care industry workers was sent a questionnaire to determine the

	Manager Initiated	Company Initiated
P E R F O R M A N C E	• Verbal praise • Personal notes • Public recognition • Spontaneous celebrations • Special privileges • Morale building meetings • Pictures and notes on bulletin boards	• Employee of the month plaques • Cash awards • Annual awards banquet • Tickets to various entertainment events • Print employee success in the company publication • Performance is major basis for promotion • Awards for good attendance records
P R E S E N C E	• Holiday parties • Gifts and cards on birthdays • Personally signed cards • Snacks • Manager has meals with employees • Manager socializes with employees • Manager greets employees as they come	• Free coffee and drinks • Annual party, picnic, or trip • Receptions for retirees • Turkey on holidays • Public advertisement of employee appreciation • Exercise facilities for employees • Hats, etc., with logo

TABLE 7.1

motivational impact of each technique on a scale of one to three with three being the highest. Ironically, manager-initiated rewards for performance came out with the highest motivational impact (2.24), but were perceived to occur with the lowest frequency. Company-initiated rewards, which have a lower motivational impact (1.82), were perceived to occur with the highest percent of frequency.

The top five motivating techniques are:

1. Manager personally congratulates employees who do a good job.
   Impact—2.73 Frequency of Use—42.3

2. Manager writes personal notes for good performance.
   Impact—2.59 Frequency of Use—24.0

3. Organization uses performance as the major basis for promotion.
   Impact—2.59 Frequency of Use—22.0

4. Manager publicly recognizes employee for good performance.
   Impact—2.41 Frequency of Use—19.4

5. Manager holds morale-building meetings to celebrate successes.
   Impact—2.20 Frequency of Use—8.0

The lowest five appreciation techniques are:

28. Organization provides items with company logo.
    Impact—1.42 Frequency of Use—23.0

27. Manager sends signed birthday cards to employees.
    Impact—1.44 Frequency of Use—10.9

26. Manager gives receptions or gifts on birthdays.
    Impact—1.50 Frequency of Use—21.0

25. Organization awards employee of the month plaque or certificate.
    Impact—1.60 Frequency of Use—26.9

24. Manager socializes with employees after work.
    Impact—1.60 Frequency of Use—32.6

Although we cannot draw conclusive evidence from one industry, with large variations in types and ages of employees and organizations, we just might stop and note that it is interesting in this, and in several other studies that what managers think employees want often differs from what they actually want. In several studies, employees rank interesting work and appreciation of a job well done as their top two desires, while managers tend to think they want good pay and job security. Perhaps in times of economic security Maslow may still be right, but the overall trend seems to suggest the opposite. Annual parties, trips, exercise facilities, and free turkeys on holidays are more costly than verbal or written praise, a smile, public recognition, and morale-building meetings, and they have the least impact. Why then, are they still the most used? In this age of quality measurement and controls, we certainly lack the appropriate research to make enlightened decisions!

8

WHERE TO BEGIN

By this point, I hope you have done some careful soul-searching about what you might be doing that is counter-productive, and about the things you haven't even begun to think about. The following chart is provided to help you to analyze where you are—so you can use the information in determining where you want to be.

RECOGNITION WORKSHEET

What specifically does your organization already do that you have previously thought of as adequate recognition?

Money:

- Our bonus, commission, and cash incentive plans.

- Where our salary fits competitively.

- Stock ownership?

- What other cash incentives do we give?

- What specifically do they recognize?

- Is it clear to employees what gets recognized with cash and how they can go about getting it?

Nonfinancial:

- Time off?

- Days or weeks of recognition?

- Public ceremonies?

- Monthly or weekly praise sessions?

- Special team award ceremonies?

- Plaques, certificates, or momentos?

- Fun or celebrations?

- Field trips?

- Special company events?

- Incentive for travel?

- Health and fitness benefits?

- Contests?

- Education benefits—both in-house and outside?

- Birthday or anniversary celebrations?

- Other?

Directly job-related

- Opportunity for advancement?

- Promoting from within?

- Increased responsibility to employees?

- Opportunities for personal growth seminars?

- How are suggestions handled?

- Frequent performance reviews (every three months)?

- System of communication in general?

- Daily communication with each employee?

What we could do that we are not now doing?

What we need to ask the employees about?

What we need to suggest to management?

Once you have a clear picture on how your organization views recognition and what is currently being done, you can begin to plan for change. By now you've discovered that recognition has to be a daily, ingrained-in-the-culture sort of thing. You cannot simply create a new program. Often, these "programs du jour" have a detrimental effect on an organization because they are usually viewed by employees as attempts to manipulate, rather than sincere efforts to appreciate.

Imagine, instead, that you are an outsider coming to view your organization for the first time. What do you see? Look at the faces. Is there a genuine sense of happiness and contentment? Have you ever really looked at the people around you? Do people seem to be friendly? Do you get a sense of excitement? What are the surroundings like? Are they stiff and formal? Or, is there a real sense of personality and style? Does everything look the same? Or, can you tell that the individuals who work here are truly unique and respected for their uniqueness? Do people greet you? Does anyone even notice your presence? Or, are they too busy to pay attention?

Listen to the conversations. Do you hear orders being drummed out? Is there one voice speaking at a meeting with all others nodding silently (or nodding off)? Are people interrupting? Or really listening? Is it obvious who's in charge? Do you hear complaints? Are most of the comments blaming or negative criticism? Or do you hear a lot of words of congratulations? Are people being celebrated? Is there laughter anywhere? Are there signs of victory and celebration? Or, is it all work and no play?

What do your internal senses tell you? Is it comfortable to work there? Do you get a feeling that people enjoy coming to work? Can you sense the camaraderie?

If your organization isn't measuring up quite yet, don't despair. And, by all means, don't just go get a program going. Changing habits takes practice. Unfortunately, no skill—indeed no "life commitment"—comes without practice and fumbling. The old adage "practice makes perfect" is more true than not. At its root is the idea that although some things do not come "naturally," repetitive and consistent use "trains" us to perform easily and automatically.

Watch children learning a sport—any sport. Some are naturals and are able to perform easily and well—at least, some aspect of the sport. Others must be lead through the fundamentals and work on the very basics. Then, they all practice. They swing the bat with "an even swing" thousands of times, they "dribble" the ball rhythmically for smoothness, they swim thousands of laps. They practice. As they practice, they correct. Soon, their muscles and nerves learn to do it right. It becomes "natural."

So, too, with *Recognition: The Quality Way.* You must be committed to "practice." And this practice may, unfortunately, be looked upon as a "program." The difference is that a program has a beginning and an end. It has a specific, (usually) measurable outcome.

Practice has only one outcome—true recognition that changes the way we interact and improves and motivates more "naturally." Instead of waiting for "upper management" or for a total program to be developed, I suggest you work on personally becoming a "recognition specialist." I am convinced that what we become, we attract, and to make a difference in an organization, you have to begin with yourself. Try the following:

Step One—Establish the Pattern

Regardless of what the entire organization is doing, or what your place is in the organization, the place to start is with yourself. Begin by getting yourself "in shape." When you begin an exercise program, you often set up specific times and actions—a half hour every other day, and an hour on Saturdays. This "set-aside" time says you are serious about making this part of your daily routine.

It is much the same with *Recognition: The Quality Way.* You must begin by establishing the pattern which will, in time, become natural. Start by looking at your calendar. You'll see meetings, schedules to be met, reviews, customer appointments, and perhaps more meetings, meetings, meetings.

Now find an open time. If one doesn't exist, make one. Take 15 minutes out of your schedule and make time for one of your employees (or peers). Now make an "appointment" to spend time with this person. Don't ask them to come to you. As much as possible, go see them. When you do, take the time to talk to them. Not necessarily about business—in fact, it is preferable not to discuss business, at first.

Sit down and talk to them as a human being. Find out about their interests; their families. Let them get to know you as well. Be sincere in your interest. Find ways to let this one person know that you are aware that he or she is a unique human being, with unique interests, needs, and wants.

If you have concerns about the business that you can share—share them. Get them to listen. By sharing, you are further acknowledging them. Everyone appreciates being confided in. We all love to feel trusted. This is not a time for corporate gossip, but for genuine human-touching-human.

Establish this as a pattern with all of your employees (as much as possible). Make time for them to show them that they matter as human beings to you. Set aside this time on your calendar as necessary time, not just something you'll do when you get around to it. See this time as valuable. Get your pattern in place and your self "in shape."

Step Two—Think Appreciation

No matter how much time you set aside for your subordinates, and no matter how much time you spend "finding out about them," nothing can replace action.

If your employees are valuable to you and your business, find ways to express it! If you need to go through personality assessments or team building exercises, do so. Get to know how each person wants to be recognized. Ask them! And then check back to see that what you give is what they meant.

Any relationship—and this IS a relationship—takes work. Decide now to end the silence and if you think it goes without saying, say it anyway. Merely "assuming" that the person understands how you feel can be a grave mistake. It is important that you make a sincere effort to express your acknowledgment of their worth to you and your business.

Read about ways other companies show appreciation. Some people like "employee-of-the-month" awards; some people want their picture and name in your organization's bulletin; some people like to be called up on stage and recognized at meetings. Don't let a week go by without finding something positive to say to everyone you work with. When you find yourself looking for things to praise instead of blame, things to praise will multiply. Get in the habit of appreciation. Remember the three-fold message: what they did, why you liked it, and how it expresses their true nature. Try doing this in the rest of your life as well—your children, your spouse or significant other, and your relatives and friends will be grateful too.

As Ken Blanchard has said, "catch people doing something right." If necessary, write these words on the top of your "to do" list each day and be sure to check it off before you leave the office each night. If you do it deliberately at first, it will also become second nature. And, I assure you, gratitude is contagious.

The most important thing is sincerity. If you don't feel that way about the people in your life, perhaps it is time to ask why. Perhaps it is time to work through the issues. But if you are to become a true recognition specialist, you must do it constantly and consistently.

If a person isn't worthy of recognition in your eyes, than, ask what you can do to help them get that way. Notice not what *they* can do, but what *you* can do. Is there clearer communication that is needed? Is it a better job description? Is it more training? Maybe they are having a personal problem and need counseling. Can you help them find it? When you assume that everyone deserves recognition, you'll find ways to help them be deserving.

Step Three—Learn to Champion Differences

Create a matrix that lists all of the people you work with on a daily or weekly basis as the rows. The columns read: tolerate, accept, celebrate, and champion. Take some time to reflect on your attitudes and feelings toward each of the people on your list and put a check mark under all the columns you can honestly say are true. Then set goals for improved communication.

Acknowledgment and acceptance are steps three and four of quality recognition. If you've done the work described above, you can't help having checks for each person in at least the first two of the above columns. Once we come to truly know another human being, it is impossible to remain indifferent about that person. Except in rare cases of severely dysfunctional behavior, we'll find something in everyone to connect with. The more we develop rapport with people, the easier it is to learn to "tolerate" the differences we find. If you come to appreciate someone's sense of humor, you lose the "edge" of annoyance for, for example, their lack of organizational skills. I know my friends have!

Have you ever noticed that after you've found a number of things to like in a person, your acceptance of their faults diminishes? We tend to do this easily when we are in love, or for members of our immediate or extended families. Now, we need to take this same attitude into the workplace.

9

How to Get the
Recognition You Deserve

With all of the seemingly wonderful incentive plans and recognition programs that exist, why is it that so many people still do not feel appreciated at work and so many more even hate their jobs? We can look to blame management, or even "the system." Of course, there is evidence to show that recognition is not among the higher priorities in many businesses today. Most companies leave recognition as an afterthought—if it is thought of at all. It seems they don't even have a clue as to where to begin. Putting this knowledge aside for a moment, in this chapter, I want to change the focus and look at the situation from another angle—the personal one. Simply put, the recognition a person receives is not dependant upon others, but is directly related to his or her ability to receive it. To truly receive recognition, we have to stop looking outside ourselves and blaming someone else for not giving us what we believe we want and start looking at our own capacity to receive.

The truth is, a cup can only be filled to its capacity. We can only receive in life what we believe we are worthy of receiving. We always receive as much as we truly allow. All of us want more recognition. Most of us don't know what we need to do to get it. And some don't get it because they don't feel like they deserve it, or they are afraid if they get something, it will be taking from someone else. Our minds, our perceptions of reality, actually create the reality we experience. If we aren't receiving what we want in life, we can look outside ourselves and blame "them"— our bosses, our parents, our spouses. Or, we can look within and see what we are doing to hold onto the current situation in our lives. There are a lot of beliefs that prevent people from receiving what they most want. For many of us, it is often easier to focus on giving than on receiving. And, now that we've spent the last eight chapters doing just that, we may be making comfortable lists about what "they" need to do to change. Now it's time to shift the focus for a while and concentrate on ourselves and how to create the beliefs and behaviors that will get us the recognition we desire and deserve.

BELIEFS

Let's begin with our beliefs about recognition. You can't give what you don't have. How can I be a person who gives recognition to another, when I am secretly jealous of the other, or feeling emptied by the giving? Sometimes we keep the very thing we want away from us because of hidden beliefs or attitudes we may have about "having." For example, most people say they want more money. Many even claim that they desire wealth. Yet, listen to their conversations. They are replete with things like, "I wonder how he got all that money? There's no way it could all be legitimate." Or, "Rich people are selfish and snobby. Who does she think she is?" Why would you want to be someone you dislike so much? I once attended a seminar where we looked at our old beliefs about money. We acted out situations where people lavishly poured money over us. Many people in the room were saying things like, "Wait, I don't deserve this." "I haven't worked hard enough for it." "You can't just give to me without my doing something in return." Others began hoarding everything that was poured on them and even began to clutch at money that was supposed to be shared with the rest of the group. "There won't be enough for me if I give it to you." "Why should I give this to you; tell me why you deserve it more than me?" The experience was revealing! Our language gives our true beliefs away and holds the clue to why we do not yet have anything in our lives which we claim we want. Recognition is no exception.

Listen to the comments you make when you receive something. Do you brush off compliments with "It was nothing," or "This old thing; I got it at a bargain basement." "I do this with my eyes closed." "It's nothing special, anyone could do what I do." Or, when you receive a compliment are you able to say, "Thank you, yes I know." If that sounds pompous, you have some thinking to do about yourself and how well you are able to receive.

Listen to the comments you make when someone else is recognized. Do you hear yourself comparing, criticizing, or complaining? Or can you boast of the genuine feeling of joy in another's triumphs? The attitude we have about others being recognized can be quite revealing in why we have or haven't been receiving recognition ourselves. Taking joy in another's achievements is one way of allowing ourselves to be open to receive what we want. Outwardly applauding or smiling when another is recognized is not enough. What is truly going on inside—both consciously and unconsciously—can give us the clue as to our own ability to receive our own recognition.

In addition to listening to what we say about others, we can also take a look at what we don't. How well do you recognize others? Once again, it's important to look at the attitude as well as the actions. We may be saying all the right words and yet feeling envy or jealousy. (Envy is wanting what the other person has and wanting them not to have it; jealousy is wishing we could have it as well.) In either case, we are focused on what is lacking in our lives rather than on the abundance. Any success teacher will tell you that what you focus on is what you will achieve. So, if our focus is on, "you have and I don't," that is, on lack, what we create in our lives is more lack. If we truly are freely focusing on the good that we are recognizing in another, that good will increase and will come our way as well. Our attitudes and beliefs create our reality. It's that simple. And that profound.

BEHAVIORS

Just changing attitudes is one piece of the picture. Some of us need to change behaviors as well. I'd hate to tell you how many thank you notes have gone unwritten in my life. You know, the thought was there, but I never followed through! And yet, I am always delighted when someone shows me the courtesy of sending a thanks. It's a simple, but sobering lesson.

So, you do send thank yous. Next, ask yourself when was the last time you really took the time to acknowledge someone at work or at home for some small thing when it wasn't mandated by company policy or by a special occasion? Remember that it's the people who we work with or live with on a daily basis that we most often overlook.

As a teacher, I noticed once that I had been particularly critical of my students' writing and speaking abilities. My intention has always been to help them to improve. I've learned over the years what makes someone a good writer or speaker and I want to share in a semester what I have learned in a lifetime. I used to give train-the-trainer seminars, and I prided myself in being paid well to tell people off! Positive critiquing is quite a talent, and most of the time I do it well. But, there have been enough times when my students have let me know in their evaluations that they were hearing messages of "not good enough" or even of "no good." This was never my intention. It's not usually the intention of parents or supervisors either, but we need to take heed if most of our comments are negative rather than positive. Inspite of our best intentions, we are often adding to the already damaged self-esteem of so many of our employees, partners, and peers. I'm glad they were so honest with me; I've been so much more careful of what I say since then!

Sometimes (and this is especially true for certain personality types), we have the attitude that the other person knows when they look good, have done a good job or had a good idea. We think to ourselves, consciously or unconsciously, that they do not need to hear anything from us. They are, after all, self-motivated. We err here more by silence than anything else. In fact, oftentimes, we find ourselves doing the opposite of what we really intend. No positive reinforcement is often interpreted as negative.

This happens all too often in the workplace. And sometimes it gets even worse. When managers assume that employees "know" they are appreciated, the only recognition they give is reprimand. Unfortunately, many people today tend to give what I would call, recognition by default. If I don't tell you you are doing something wrong, you can assume that you are doing an okay job. Many of us have come from homes where silence was the norm. We knew when things were not going well, but we didn't quite have a measure for normal. Or, maybe we never had the real assurance that it was great that we were alive and that just our being here was a cause for celebration. So many children—now adults—face the world with a core belief that they were unwanted and that somehow they didn't or don't belong, or even don't have a right to live. They try to perform for the recognition they never got from their parents and probably will never get. Of course, for the average "well-adjusted" adult, this is more subtle than overt. But that's just the problem. Too many of us lived in homes where love remained unexpressed and communication, at it's best, was centered around problems or chaos situations. The literature on dysfunction speaks of breaking that silence. In organizational settings, that has several implications.

Am I asking us to play psychologist or psychiatrist as managers? Somewhat. Part of our training in business needs to include the ability to face what we are seeking ourselves so that our communications can be less narcissistic. A long time ago, for example, I recognized my own need for applause, and so I frequently put myself in situations where I get it! Too many people don't even acknowledge the needs that they themselves have and it comes out in covert rather than overt behavior. Self-esteem issues must be addressed as part of every seminar and meeting in the workplace today. We need to learn to facilitate and understand process and emotions as well as content and ideas. We have to stop pretending that we are all self-actualized beings. It is time to acknowledge our wholeness as human beings, or rather our process of becoming whole. Too often we separate who we are as people in our home and social life from who we behave as at work. Many people today are aware of their need for support and are working on changing dysfunctional behavior at home, but then come to work and have to pretend that none of the dysfunction exists. No wonder there are so many unhappy people. And, it's been proven time and time again that happy people are more productive. We can't stop working to sit around and share our stories all day, but we do need to acknowledge that we are multifaceted, multilevel human beings who are filling roles and accomplishing tasks together. And, sometimes we are not functioning in the most adult capacity and are experiencing old childhood hurts and needs.

In the quality movement, we are asking people to work together as fully functioning teams *assuming* that we are fully functioning individuals. Short of the enlightened avatars and masters, none of us are! Communication at a needs level is something organizations are beginning to learn to acknowledge as necessary. Recognition is about feeling seen, heard, and understood. When we don't know how to communicate properly, we often resort to silence. Healthy communication is essential to recognition. Silence is not the answer.

The now famous Abilene Paradox addresses another aspect of this issue of silence. This management paradox is based on a true story set in Abilene, TX. A family was sitting on a porch one Sunday afternoon when someone suggested that they take a drive to Abilene for dinner. No one really wanted to go, but everyone did because no one wanted to be the one in disagreement. The meal was mediocre at best, and the drive was long and hot in a car without air conditioning. Everyone was miserable, but no one spoke. Basically, because no one spoke up, everyone did what no one wanted to do.

In our organizations, we clearly are guilty of this. The problem is not one of conflict resolution; it's more one of agreement resolution! Everyone agrees that something is not the way it should be, but no one speaks. How many projects go through the drafting board when no one believes they really will work? How many plans are made and goals set that everyone agrees are unrealistic, but no one voices dissent? We agree more often than disagree, but we remain in silent ignorance of it.

It would be nice if every person in authority knew how to communicate and could clearly set expectations and then do periodic and sometimes surprise performance appraisals to let people know they were on track. Managers often use the "too busy" excuse, or, "it's their job," or some variation of the same. What are we busy about anyway? Have we missed the essential for the urgent? Is it that they are really too busy to recognize others, that they don't want to, or simply that they don't know how. The truth is, often managers themselves are not being given the recognition they want or need and as I hinted at above, "you can't give what you don't have."

Anne Wilson Schaef, in her books on addiction in society and in organizations, underlines this dilemma. Many behavior patterns that we see in work are the same that have come out of the addictive patterns that are the result of relating to alcoholics or other substance abusers. Unfortunately, this scenario is more prevelant than we like to acknowledge. And, whether the manager is the abuser, or the codependent that supports and allows the behavior, or even encourages it, what is usually set up is a cycle of silence or covert communication at best. Here's the silence once again!

Paula Bernstein, in her book *Family Ties/Corporate Bonds* (Doubleday, 1985), describes how family roles are acted out in the workplace. She suggests that the workplace recreates the family environment, and we all take on roles of fathers, mothers, sisters, and brothers. Of course, a lot of this remains at the unconscious level. Several studies have appeared in business magazines in the last few years, claiming that anywhere from 90% to 96% of the population suffer from addiction, or are the codependents to the addicted person. Communication among these classes of people is at best awkward. Those who are under the influence of an addiction cannot always communicate directly and codependents are known to read into and make assumptions on what other people have said. It is amazing that any direct communication takes place at all. Our organizations need to acknowledge this and offer the necessary training and perhaps counseling or other intervention to support the change toward quality relationships at work. Quality products cannot be produced when the quality of the relationships of the people responsible for producing them is lacking. When relationships are suffering, recognition is nonexistent.

It's no wonder then that we feel a lack of recognition. Much of our behavior has been focused on protecting ourselves from the dysfunction. Those who have entered into recovery programs or have taken seminars that support direct communication are learning that it is possible to ask for and to get needs met. They are learning that it's time to move beyond blame and shame and get to a point beyond pointing a finger at parents—or authority figures that have come to represent parents. To get the recognition you want, need, and deserve, you have to begin by taking responsibility for your own needs and stop looking for it to come from mom, dad, or the boss! If you are not getting the kind of recognition that you want, it is time to do some self-parenting in this area and give it, first of all, to yourself.

How do we give ourselves the recognition we deserve and seem to want from others? First, we need to really get honest about our beliefs. We already saw what some of them might be. If we don't believe we are worthy or worthwhile, we may need to find a support group or therapist to help us. We all need to start off knowing we deserve recognition just because we are, not only for the things we do. If we feel we just need a tune-up in this area, we can begin by listing our strengths and good qualities—we all have them. Yet, we tend so often to focus on the faults, the things that we do wrong, and the aspects of ourselves that we label less than perfect. Remember, what we focus on increases. So each day we need to take time out to let ourselves know that we accept and approve of ourselves exactly as we are. I suggest doing it in front of a mirror. If you find it difficult to do, you need to do it twice each day!

What we need to do is to *recognize*, that is, change our minds about the truth of who we are. We need to begin to use the stop button on the recorders that we've been playing for years and play a new tape—the ones that are used by the people who have overcome. When you begin to think that you are not getting enough recognition, think again. Change what you were thinking about yourself and see if under the belief: "No one else sees who I am and what I do," is the real message: "I don't see who I am and what I do—but am still seeing who I was and what I've done." The exciting thing about thoughts is that it is always possible to have a new one and when we change our thinking, we literally change our experience and therefore our lives. We become what we think about most often. So, when we think thoughts of lack, we create lack. When we recognize these thoughts, we get to see that that we live in an abundant universe and that our good is there for the asking. Yes, we must learn who to ask and how—but first we must learn to believe that it is true!

To counteract tapes of negative things, we can reprogram our thinking with the truth. Find ways to repeat affirmative things over and over again during your day. You can deliberately use positive reinforcement on yourself. Anyone who has even seen Tony Robbins, (famed fire walker and success seminar leader) "perform," knows what I mean. He has a way of snapping his arm and yelling "YES" each time he comes on stage or is ready to do something breakthrough. He teaches that this helps put him in a favorable "state" where he remembers to feel good about himself. His arm snapping serves as a reminder of all the times he has been successful and links this next experience among those successes. We've all had some positive experience we can anchor ourselves with. We can create our own sign or symbol or mental habit of feeling good. It will serve as a far better habit than the one many of us have—correcting ourselves and belittling ourselves as "stupid" or "dumb" everytime we do something less than perfect. Find a saying or a movement that will work for you and start changing the negative self-talk into more positive affirmations.

I have a friend who has learned to look in the mirror when she makes a mistake and sing a version of "I've made a mistake and I'm beautiful, I'm beautiful . . ." Isn't that a wonderful attitude for all of us to take through life?

Reinforcing ourselves is something we often neglect. Perhaps we were taught it was pride and we needed to be "humbled," or perhaps it just doesn't occur to us, or we demand too much of ourselves. As a result, we go for days on end, moving from project to project, unthanked by ourselves. This kind of self-deprivation is a prominent factor in anxiety and depression. We have to learn to give to ourselves before we can truly receive anything we want from another. Each of us have to discover the unique ways that we can do that. Find a method that works for you.

If you don't feel comfortable singing to yourself or you can't find or can't imagine yourself using a mirror, at least award yourself with an hour off, a walk or talk with friends, or whatever else would indicate your own self-approval. The performer Ruth Gordon was once heard to say, "An actor has to have compliments. If I go long enough without getting a compliment, I compliment myself, and that's just as good, because at least then I know it's sincere."

We can find other ways of acknowledging ourselves by exploring other facets of the word recognition. There are many ways we can look at recognition. One definition of the word is "to have a current knowing of something that happened before—to know again." Isn't that what we do when we celebrate? We bring to our minds something that has already taken place so that we can reexperience the emotions of joy and delight in a work well done. If we're going to replay old tapes, why not replay the positive ones, making them louder, brighter, clearer and stronger in our memory? The anchoring example above reinforces this. Yet, sometimes we use this against ourselves. Many of us don't recognize our own capabilities because we allow ourselves to be defined by the experiences we labeled negative in our past. If something doesn't go right once, we accept it, but when it happens two or three times, we begin to give ourselves labels and say things like, "I'm not good at . . ." "I never . . ." or "I can't . . ." You complete the appropriate sentence. One of the major steps necessary in achieving more recognition is to discover and replace the self-denigrating messages you are currently using on yourself. Just fill in the blanks on the three suggested above for starters and see where your self-esteem is going lately.

There is a principle that successful people use that would serve us well here when and if we find ourselves uttering such negative affirmations. That is, "If anyone can do something, anyone can do it." That's a thought worth repeating and pondering. "If anyone can do something, anyone can do it." What makes us believe "we can't?" What's the difference between those who can't and those who do? Perhaps the best answer comes in the form of an old joke that appears in many forms, but always speaks the same message. In one version, a visitor from Texas, driving in a limousine and lost on New York's lower east side, asked an aged, bearded New Yorker, "How do you get to Carnegie Hall?" The famous story says he answered, "Practice."

We most often use the word "practice" as a VERB. Many of us will remember having to leave our play as children to practice a musical instrument, or the hours spent on the basketball or tennis courts, practicing foul shots or serves, or the many laps we've done in swimming pools. We practice to achieve goals, to get ahead, and to make money. We practice dancing, we practice our golf swing. We practice to learn a skill. What makes you and I different from the Olympic medal winners or the Donald Trumps of this world is that they do not believe they can't and so they see practice as a NOUN. It's not something you do, but something you have, or something you are. Winners don't practice because they have to. The truth is, they love to! What you practice on a regular basis becomes an integral part of your life. It's the path on which you travel; it's who you are. We would do well to model this type of practice.

The whole concept of modeling from neuro-linguistic programming is based on the premise that if we pattern our physiology and our thoughts after any winner, we can accomplish exactly what he or she does. Remember, "anything anyone can do. . . ." We must begin to erase the negative tapes that deep down say, "I could never" or "I'm not worthy of" being recognized, if we truly want to be. (And, if we think we don't want to be recognized by now, begin again at Chapter 1!)

We can also think about recognition as "knowing that we know" something. We delight when a child looks at a dog or cat and calls it by its proper name. We cheer when he or she can point to letters or numbers and properly announce their meaning. In these cases, we say that the child recognized something. And when that recognition is directed at us, like the first sound that remotely resembles "ma" or "da," we receive it with incredible excitement.

As adults, how many of us give ourselves credit for knowing that we know, or even allow ourselves to know that we know? So often we still hold onto the messages of

"I'm not smart enough," "good enough," "strong enough," or ". . . .enough" that come from the voices of the past that echoed, "What do you know?" or "What makes you think you know so much?" Who among us has not heard those words once too often so that, albeit unconsciously, we still believe it? Inside each of us lies the answer to every question we may have in life and the solution to every problem. Sometimes we've shut out this voice that speaks truth to us by so many other distractions both internal and external. Many of us have come to believe that the negative voices or words that we hear are more true and real than the positive ones.

And TV doesn't help us much either. We are so used to humor that is negative that we take it for granted. Almost every sitcom is replete with messages that someone is not okay. Think of the popular "Cheers," whose very theme song, "Sometimes you want to go where everybody knows your name, and their always glad you came" speaks of recognition. We all laugh at the Cliff brain jokes and the put downs on the "loser," Rebecca. The dialogue is constant put-down. And what about Saturday Night Live or the endless late night talk shows that all boast of an opening monologue, which is usually a put-down routine? It's become popular to see and find humor in the negative. Listen to our conversations, even with people we love most, and note how often the humor is negative, when we really mean to say, "you're great." "I love you." We say things like, "You look great—for a change!" "That's a great idea—where did you get it from?" We've been programmed to accept negatives more than positives. And it is easier to let a sarcastic remark slide off our tongue than it is to express what we truly feel.

Think about it. If you and I were walking down the street and in passing a store window I looked in and said, "My, don't I look attractive today. My hair is perfect; my skin is radiant. I love the way I look." You'd think I was strange or self-absorbed at best. And yet, if we passed the same mirror and I began ranking on myself and my appearance and said, "Oh I look awful, today. It's certainly a bad hair day. And look how puffy my eyes are. I need to get more sleep." You'd probably find this conversation more palatable and would think nothing of it. What's wrong with this picture? We've become a world where when we aren't silent; it is more acceptable to be negative! We need work to change this. And, that work starts with ourselves.

So, the way to assure that we will receive more recognition is to learn to recognize ourselves—who we truly are as well as what we know. First we must attune ourselves to hear the negative tapes that are playing and replace them with positive ones, and then we need to find ways of celebrating who we are. Of course, we must first be able to answer that important philosophical question. Have we spent as much time answering the question, What is my life? or What does my life wish to become? as we have spent with a business plan or proposal for a project that might have a lifespan of less than one-tenth of our own? Most organizations wouldn't dream of starting a project without some thought and planning and a fair idea of the end result that they want to achieve. No business can be launched if the owners have no purpose in mind. No book would sell that didn't have something specific to say. And yet, we often let this thing called LIFE just happen and go on from day to day without a clue as to what our true purpose is.

In traveling around the world speaking, I often ask an audience to raise their hands if they have seriously considered and written down their life purpose. With all the time-management techniques, current authors and long-standing success gurus posing that question, I am still startled to be able to count the responses on one or two hands when my sample population ranges from 500 to 2,000. I've never seen a tombstone enscribed, "I brought all projects in on time and under budget." And yet, so much of our energy—especially at work—is spent on projects rather than relationships. We move in a collective direction towards a company's end and hardly ever ask how it is serving the individual and his or her life purpose. Quality programs have begun to help organizations learn problem solving techniques and questioning skills. I still wonder—are we asking the *right* questions?

The question of life purpose brings us back to Socrates' adage, "Know thyself." It is as true today as it was then. No recognition from outside ourselves will be forthcoming or longlasting until we begin with the recognition that must come from within. For a starter, take time to find out what your life is really about. When you come to really understand your life purpose, you get a better sense of who you are, and a true understanding of the things you really want recognition for. It could be an eye-opening experience.

LIFE PURPOSE EXERCISE

If you need help, start the discovery with an exercise like the following. Begin writing a list of 10 (more or less) nouns or phrases that describe the characteristics that you like about yourself. For example, hospitality is one of mine. No, I don't serve afternoon tea on the appropriate china or make certain that my guests have everything they need when entering my house. But, people are comfortable in my presence. I'm the kind of person that strangers ask directions from and people on airplanes tell of their upcoming promotion or latest marital crisis. Classes I teach get comfortable right away. I like this quality about me. I call it hospitality. Some others are compassion, sensuality, creativity, sense of humor ... I'm talking about you now too! You get the idea. Create your own list now.

When that's complete, begin to create a list of ways you like to express yourself. It's best to write these as gerunds. Remember those? They are nouns used as verbs that end in -ing, like: teaching, speaking, mothering, fathering, problem-solving, nuturing, dancing, skiing, singing ... Stop here and do this now.

The third step is to write a one-sentence or phrase description of your vision for a perfect world (and it doesn't have to be perfect)—just allow whatever comes in a stream-of-consciousness thought to be written on paper.

Next, put a star next to the three most important items on each of the first two lists. Not necessarily the first ones written, but the ones you would write if you were doing a personal ad and wanted to make sure you had the most important pieces intact.

Now, we'll put it all together. Fill in the blanks of the following sentence:
The purpose of my life is to use my _____ , _____ , and _____ by _____ ,_____ , and _____ , so that _____.
The first three blanks are to be filled in with the three items you starred on the first list, the next three from the second, and the final line is your vision for a perfect world.

Once you have written this out, feel free to massage it and make changes so that it sounds smooth and truly reflects who you believe you are. Most people who have done this exercise find it quite accurate. Perhaps you have found that what you are now doing fits perfectly into your life purpose. If so, you are among the fortunate ones and are ready to move on to step two. If not, is it any wonder that you do not feel recognized at work. When you have a sense that your very purpose of being is one thing and what you are doing with your life is another, you are lacking congruence and may never feel truly appreciated. Usually what we want to be appreciated for are the things we list in our life purpose, and if what we are doing is so far removed from the truth of who we are, it would be hard to find anyone else who could really understand your need when you are not expressing it by your life!

Once you understand your life purpose, and feel that you are on track in living according to it, the next step is to really see what your values are. You can do this simply by asking yourself the question, What's really important to me in life? Or in a job? Or you can ask the question, How do I spend my free time? or What do I spend my money on? What do these things give me? Keep asking these questions and simply record the answers that come to you. When you feel that you have written a sufficient list, begin to put them in priority order. If you could only have one, what would it be, and so on. Be sure that what you list are values and not tangible things. "My family," or "money" should not be on the list, because both of those things represent something deeper to you. They are not ends in themselves, but means to an end (e.g., a sense of security, or joy, or love, or freedom, or purpose).

When your list is complete, I'd suggest talking these over with your partner or friend or coworkers to see what they tell you further about yourself. Many people think one thing is important to them, and when they go to make out a list like this, find out that something else is really more valuable. The things we most value are the things we want to have recognition around. If I value honesty above all else, when someone lies to me, they lose my respect. If that same person tries to acknowledge my work or my appearance, or whatever, there is no way I can truly hear and accept what they have to say, because I listen to compliments through an integrity filter.

First you learn what your life purpose and values are. This gives you a good indication of what it is you want to be recognized for. And, once you know, write it down and speak it out. The world has a unique system of checks and balances. "What goes around, comes around." "Bread cast upon the waters . . ." There's a universal law of circulation. You will get what you put out. When you are giving a speech, for example, you get the best evaluation when you ask for feedback on something specific. Through my years of training trainers, I have learned that in fact, the only feedback we ever really learn from, is the feedback we specifically ask for. (Remember this when it comes to the next performance appraisal you either give or receive!) The same applies in work and in home life. So often we expect others to mind-read what it is that we want or what is important to us.

There's a trap that so many people fall into when they say they want someone else to anticipate their needs without telling them what they are. Then, we punish the other person for not knowing what we didn't tell them. It's a game we sometimes play, but it's one that doesn't get us what we want, so it's time to give up playing it. Years ago, I used to be chagrined when certain friends didn't remember my birthday. Many of them had grown up in homes where birthdays just weren't that special. I learned to tell my friends that my birthday is important to me, and now I get lots of calls and cards at the end of November! This is a small personal example. But it illustrates what we attempt to do both at home and in the workplace. We expect that people will "see" what is important to us; we want our bosses, our peers, and our friends to be psychics and then to give us just what we need. Usually, they are too busy trying to get their own needs met to notice when ours aren't, so if we want recognition for something specific, we need to find ways of asking for it. It's a question of silence and learning to communicate needs.

When you ask for something, put it in terms of the other person's wants and needs instead of your own. Every salesperson and marketer knows that the most important station on everyone's mind is WIIFM—what's in it for me. So, we want to learn to ask for what we need in a way that will serve the other's needs as well.

Many of my students have taken these ideas about recognition and given them to their bosses! In every case, they've been called in and told, "I hear you. What is it you would like me to notice more?" And what followed was an honest conversation, usually about the need to have a certain aspect of their work or their talent recognized. In each case, they told their supervisor that they wanted to help him or her with the task of appraisals. When appraisals aren't forthcoming, we can gripe that we don't know where we stand, or we can take responsibility for ourselves and ASK. And if that doesn't work, it might be time to ask ourselves why we stay in situations where our needs aren't getting met? Old stuff again, perhaps? We do need to knock on doors that have something behind it. Many of us go to dry wells to get water and wonder why our thirst is still there. We need to ask for what we want, but we also must be certain that we are asking the right person (i.e., someone who is capable of giving it to us). Sometimes we think we want something at work that is really missing at home or we demand from our managers what we want from our spouses. It's worth looking at.

TAKING ACTION

Although it is true that we must first change any beliefs we may have that block us from receiving the recognition we want and deserve, believing alone doesn't make it so. I'm sure you've heard it said that if wishes were things, all children would ride ponies! So, in addition to changing beliefs, we often have to change some actions or behaviors as well. The first action we all need to take is learning to ask for what we want and knowing who to ask it from.

In addition to asking directly for what you want, what are some of the practical day-to-day things you can do to experience more recognition? The place to start with any new belief is in the practical level of experience. What follows is a list of very pragmatic suggestions for those of you who may have trouble asking directly but who truly want to begin to become more visible. You'll find doing any or all of these helpful. At least you can know that you are taking the first step in receiving the ultimate recognition you desire and deserve.

1. Begin by finding all the possible ways you can to praise others. Each day, be sure that at least one telephone call and one memo includes a positive pat on the back to the person with whom you are communicating. If you already do this much, make it five calls and memos. You might find you can say something positive in EVERY transaction. Just be sure it is sincere. You'll find it easy once you start looking for things to praise and you may begin to notice all the blaming you are currently doing. Changing each blame thought to one of praise will make you a more positive and happier person. And other people always notice. You'll find out that it is contagious.

I recall a story about a man in New York who decided to take on this practice. The first person he met for the day was a taxicab driver who drove him to work. He complimented the man on the safe and quick ride and the cab driver who had been quiet and sullen, suddenly perked up and began a pleasant conversation. He then began to visualize his positive message going from that man to each person who entered the taxi that day. His positive attitude was certainly multiplied.

2. Offer your services and make it known that you want to participate in things that are beyond your normal job requirements. If your company is already part of a total quality effort, you can offer to lead a special interest group or focus group or become the leader of a cross-functional team. There are always special task forces for special projects. You might even create one that no one has though of yet. If this is something you have not done previously, you'll have to push beyond your current limits. Isn't that what you want? Aren't you getting limited attention now? To get more, you'll have to push the limits.

If you are the person who always volunteers, you can do something different as well. Become the quiet supporter of a person who doesn't usually get the limelight. Work behind the scenes to get information for someone else. Do the homework in private and let someone else shine in public. The surest way to success in any endeavor is to help other people come to success.

3. If you can, find ways of getting involved in community service in a way that you can promote your company outside the workplace. Think about ways of getting the company positive press and recognition, and a natural follow-on will be your own. Be sure to get involved in something that you love. Help the environment; save the whales; work with abused children; become a big brother or big sister. Find something you can do at least a few hours every week. There are volunteer organizations in every community that are longing for your help.

Even if your company never finds out, you'll have done yourself the biggest favor. We don't serve in order to get recognized but we'll never serve without it. It's a natural consequence.

4. Find ways to contribute to charitable organizations. You may discover talents you never knew you had. Giving always begets receiving. It's the natural cycle of things. They are like two sides of the same coin. One cannot happen without the other. And, besides, most charitable organizations do a really good job of recognizing their volunteers! We can learn a great deal if we study them and learn to treat our employees like volunteers in the process.

5. Attend training, return to school, go for a new certification, or get involved in personal development seminars. Anything you can do to foster your own self-actualization will also foster your being seen and noticed and appreciated. You'll be a more interesting person; you'll meet new people and expand your horizons. Become a life-long learner. When you increase the things you know, you increase the things you can get known for and it gives you the opportunity to really appreciate others who are experts in fields in which you may yet be a novice. Exposing yourself to new people and new ideas can go a long way in stimulating your creativity. Once you open the door to one discovery, you'll find that doors keep opening. Open doors lead to open minds and the open mind is certainly more ready to receive than the closed one.

6. Get involved in networking groups. There are always plenty of volunteer jobs to be done and networking groups all have newsletters where you can get some publicity if that is appropriate. Again, find

the one that fits your interests and needs. In my town, there's a group that meets for breakfast, lunch, or dinner on every day of the week. If you learn how to network well, you'll master the art of asking for what you want, and you'll easily be able to find the right person to ask for whatever you need. This alone is a valuable lesson.

7. Take a more active part in meetings at work. You might consider acting as the recorder who keeps the minutes and then be sure your name is on the copy that is sent to all participants. Or, act as the scribe during the meeting. As people discuss key points or ideas, you put them up on the flipchart or board and unconsciously, people begin to associate you with the positive ideas you are writing!

If time permits, review meeting agendas in advance and offer to provide research, information, or other data for participants. Or, come with copies of a pertinant article for the other members to read. It may seem like a small thing, but others will appreciate it and remember it as well.

You might even consider taking on challenging or a risky task that was discussed at the meeting. When was the last time you volunteered to do whatever was being requested? Your name will be recorded in the minutes and it will be noted, I promise you.

Or, if any of the above is further than you are comfortable, volunteer to be the timekeeper. Your voice will continually be heard but it will be less risky than having it be your opinions or ideas. Those will come next. If you are not being heard, remember, you can't expect other people to read your mind.

Meetings are a great place to be seen and heard. Whatever you have done before, be a little out of character next time. Do something you wouldn't have done before.

8. Ask for the special assignments. I know you have enough to do already, but if what you are already doing isn't getting you what you want and need, the simple answer is to do something else! See above.

9. Orchestrate a support group or work team that addresses issues in the workplace. Take on leadership in this "informal" environment. Many companies provide opportunities for lunchtime "brown-bag" meetings or after hour get-togethers. Use these as an opportunity to assert yourself and be noticed. If you have public speaking ability, volunteer to be a guest speaker on a topic you think might be of interest to others. It's a chance to give your opinions and be heard as the expert.

10. Share the books, videos, and audios that have helped you in your professional and personal development with others. Circulate a recommended reading list to your department or entire company. Be sure to include your name and telephone number as a contact source. You might even want to summarize some of these for your coworkers and managers. I have seen people do this quite successfully. When you summarize something you have read, people automatically assume that you are well read and intelligent. These same people then get called on for the special projects and more visible assignments, and ultimately, the promotions and raises as well.

11. Volunteer to learn new skills, techniques, or jobs. In this age of diversification and team play, it's important that you know the other person's work as well as your own. You'll be much more valuable to the company, and you'll feel a sense of accomplishment at your own progress. Surveys have shown that people are happiest at jobs where they feel they have an opportunity to keep learning. Don't wait for someone to give you the opportunity. One of the most frequent mistakes that employees make is to assume that the responsibility for their development lies with their manager or with the company. It is not ultimately up to management to see that you are happy and fulfilled. It is up to you. Take a proactive role in your own development.

12. Once you have learned other skills, if it is at all possible with what you are currently doing, take over an extra workload for someone going on vacation or leave of absence. If you do this on a temporary basis, you may find yourself opening up new doors and opportunities that you never knew existed. We sometimes work alongside of people for years and never know exactly what they do. The more people and work you get to know, the more you will find yourself being known.

13. Maintain a positive, energetic, and enthusiastic attitude in general. Everyone wants to associate with a "winner." Keep a mirror (there it is again!) near your desk or phone and notice how you look while you work. It is a fact that when you change your state, you change how you feel. It is impossible to feel depressed with a constant smile on your face. Try walking down the hall smiling at people and see if "the whole world smiles with you." It's a sure

way to feel good. Sometimes just being smiled at can change the way you feel about yourself. A smile is one of the cheapest and easiest means of recognition, and one in our too busy world that we often forget.

14. Be proactive with managers about feedback. Ask for it when it doesn't come your way. But then, be sure you are willing to hear what is being said. Develop an attitude that accepts yourself exactly where you are while being constantly open for improvement. Ask yourself frequently, "Am I ready and willing to change?" If who you are now is not creating the recognition that you want in your life, there's something you need to change. Be open to hear what that something is and then be willing to do it. Use every opportunity for growth.

15. Write articles for your company newsletter, or industry trade journals. Publications are always looking for good articles. It helps if you write well, but you don't have to be a world expert—that's what editors are for!

If you don't have original ideas for stories, why not consider interviewing someone who does? Years ago, I became a monthly columnist in a worldwide trade magazine in an industry that I knew little about, simply by interviewing people who did. My name was on the masthead and months after I had stopped writing the column, people were still calling me and acknowledging something they had read that they enjoyed. I was getting recognized for writing about something somebody else did. I was then able to pass on the praise to the person who I had written about and the cycle of recognition continued.

16. Invite people for breakfast or lunch to "pick their brain" on their expertise. Most people love to share their knowledge and you'll be viewed as someone who wants to learn. You don't have to start with the company president. Although, you'll be surprised at how many would love the opportunity to meet with you. Find someone you casually say hello to in the hall and start there. You can start interdepartmental communication this way. I know some people who have tried this and incredible ideas came from this informal sharing. They found themselves doing more systems-type thinking because they now had access to information and people that they had never been involved with before.

SOME SUMMARY PRINCIPLES

If you find yourself saying "I can't do that" to all of the above, take a look again at your belief systems. Why CAN'T you? Is it them, out there? Or, is there something you need to revisit, rethink, and realign? There's a famous definition of insanity—when we continue to do the same thing over and over and expect different results. If the results you are getting on your job are not what you want, do something different!

Remember that recognition on the job doesn't have to come only from the top. Find ways that you can recognize from the bottom up as well. Forget the old "apple polisher" label and look for ways you can support the people above you. If you are genuine in your efforts and comments, everyone will appreciate it. When you make them look good, they appreciate it in return. And when they feel appreciated and acknowledged, they are more apt to give it to the others who work for them as well, so you will have done your peers a great service.

One of the places we often forget to get and give recognition is to our peers. Although it is nice to be recognized by the company president or by an immediate supervisor, deep down all of us have an even greater need to be respected and accepted by our peers. I know of several companies that make peer recognition goals and actually have these goals become part of their formal appraisal system. I wouldn't want to see praise given just so you can get a good appraisal, but the idea that we are judged on the basis of how we find the good in others, is really part of a universal truth. Truly, everything we give to another is really given to ourselves. We might ask ourselves, "Are we demanding what we are unwilling or unable to give?" It's a principle of the universe that we only get what we give out. It's a fact of life. What we give out always comes back to us. It may not come from the same person we give to or in the manner that we expect, but we can be certain that there will be a cause and effect result.

So, without being codependant and without doing it to get something back, become a person who cares enough to find out who another really is, and take the time to appreciate what the other does. As Jean Houston said in *The Possible Human* (J.P. Tucker, 1982), "A look that goes straight to another's soul can charge that life with new meaning. Something tremendous awakens which allows a person to release years of hurt or denigration." We have tremendous power within us to be healers of humanity. And what we give out comes back to us a hundredfold.

Therefore, never criticize another before you have walked in his or her mocassins for awhile. Never flatter. Be sure what you are saying to another is sincere. Never condemn another. Be sure what you are saying about another is not only true, but also necessary and kind. Take time to find out how others can feel like they are getting what they want. If we approach one another as extensions of ourselves, we'll always make the extra effort to listen and make the attempt to figure out what the real needs are or why another does what he or she does. When you eliminate judgment of others, you eliminate judgment of yourself. When you take this basic approach to life, you will be the kind of person everyone wants to be around and recognition will be a natural consequence.

One personal quality that everyone would do well to develop more is an attitude of gratitude. What we focus on in life increases. People who show gratitude are those who recognize the glass as half-full rather than half-empty. We may actually be receiving more than we realize. One year, I decided to focus on how much I really receive in life. Whenever someone offered to do something for me, large or small, I said yes. What an eye-opening practice. I got to observe how often in the past I had denied another the pleasure of giving by the brush off words, "Oh, don't bother, I can do that myself," or "Let me do that." I became aware of how often I shut off my receiving valve. After that 40-day experiment, I began to also learn to receive more graciously and to even accept a compliment more easily and became aware of how often people offer to give me help or give me praise. Sometimes when I don't feel recognized, it's because I have blinded myself to the many ways I am. Most of us receive recognition often— people are trying to get through to love us, and we shut them out. As we open our eyes, ears, and perhaps our hearts more fully, we may have new experiences.

Although we are looking AT the recognition that is being proffered to us, however, we have to be certain not to be looking FOR it! This principle may sound like it contradicts what I have already said, but then who ever said life was free of contradictions? To get recognition, you have to not want it. You've got to not want it to get it. When you look for it, you'll never find it. It's all about letting things happen rather than making them happen. No one forces the sun to rise, and it's hard to keep that from happening. Wanting something is an admission that you do not yet have it. Allowing it to happen is another story. There is a paradox that works in this universe, the only way to truly have something is to let it be. When you look for recognition, it's like looking for love, it eludes you. When you stop looking for it, it appears everywhere.

Finally, to get recognition all of the time, realize that we are all ONE anyway. This is a principle at the heart of both Eastern and Western spirituality and is also a newly expressed idea of quantum physics! We are all connected, every cell or atom that is now a part of me, was perhaps a part of you at one time. We are all connected. If you win, I win too. So, when another is given the award or applause that you may have coveted for yourself, know that when you have reached a point in life where you know that all is one, it won't matter what part gets there first. When corporations in America get that message, our economy will change, our experience of work will change, and our lives will change accordingly. Manufacturing cannot exist without research and development and information systems wouldn't have information if it wasn't for shipping and production. We need to change our paradigms. We are not a machine that has separate parts. We are more like a hologram where the whole is contained in each of the parts. When we start to do more "systems thinking," and recognize the inherent truth of our oneness, better quality of products will be one result, but better quality of life will be even more evident.

How well do we take pride in another's success as if it were our own? What are often called "stage parents" do this to a fault. They live vicariously through their children, wanting them to be all they themselves never were, or wanting them to have the things they never did. This isn't the kind of pride I am speaking of. When we genuinely experience our oneness, we will begin to know that everything I give is a gift to myself and anything anyone receives is also a gift to me. Most of us have a way to go before we can get to this level of thinking—but the results are worth aiming for! Hope you'll join me in the process.

SUGGESTED READING

CHAPTER 1

Blanchard, K. (1990). *The One Minute Manager.* New York: Morrow.

Freudenberger, H. (1980). *Burn-Out: The High Cost of High Achievement.* New York: Anchor Press.

Carnegie, Dale. (1936). *How to Win Friends & Influence People.* New York: Simon & Schuster.

Champagne, Paul, J., & McAfee, R. Bruce. (1989). *Motivating Strategies for Performance and Productivity: A Guide to Human Resource Development.* Westport, CT: Quorum Books.

Covey, S. (1990). *Seven Habits of Highly Effective People.* New York: Summit Books.

Covey, S. (1991). *Principle-Centered Leadership.* New York: Summit Books.

Drucker, Peter. (1992). *Managing for the Future.* New York: Harper and Row.

Drucker, Peter. (1985). *Innovation and Entrepreneurship.* New York: Harper and Row.

Drucker, P. (1980). *Managing in Turbulent Times.* New York: Harper & Row.

Harris, T. George. (1993). "The Post-Capitalist Executive: An Interview with Peter F. Drucker." pp. 115–122. *Harvard Business Review.*

Herzberg, Frederick. (1990). "One More Time: How Do You Motivate Employees?" *Harvard Business Review.*

Hersey, P. and Blanchard, K.H. (1993). *Management of Organizational Behavior.* Englewood Cliffs, NJ: Prentice-Hall.

Houston, J. (1982). *The Possible Human.* New York: J.P. Tarcher/Houghton Mifflin.

Iacocca, L. (1984). *Iacocca: An Autobiography.* New York: Bantam.

Maslow, A. (1976). *The Farther Reaches of Human Nature.* New York: Penguin.

Mayo, E. (1977). *The Human Problems of an Industrial Civilization.* Salem, NH: Ayer Company.

Peters, T. (1991). *Thriving on Chaos: Handbook for a Management Revolution.* New York: Harper Perennial.

Progoff, I. (1975). *At a Journal Workshop.* Los Angeles: J.P. Tarcher.

Pryor, K. (1984). *Don't Shoot the Dog.* New York: Simon & Schuster.

Senge, Peter. (1990). *The Fifth Discipline.* New York: Doubleday.

Skinner, B.F. (1974). *About Behaviorism.* New York: Knopf.

Zaleznik, Abraham. (1990). *Executive's Guide to Motivating People.* Chicago: Bonus Books.

CHAPTER 2

Bennis, W. (1985). *The Planning of Change.* New York: Harper & Row.

Bridges, W. (1980). *Transitions: Making Sense of Life's Changes.* Reading, MA: Addison-Wesley.

Brookfield, S.D. (1987). *Developing Critical Thinkers.* San Francisco: Jossey-Bass.

Cell, E. (1984). *Learning to Learn from Experience.* Albany: State University of New York.

Fingarette, H. (1963). *The Self of Transformation.* New York: Harper.

Goodman, E. (1979). *Turning Points: How People Change Through Crisis and Commitment.* Garden City, NY: Doubleday.

Gould, R.L. (1978). *Transformation: Growth and Change in Adult Life.* New York: Simon & Schuster.

Guest, R.H., Hersey, P. and Blanchard, K.H. (1986). *Organizational Change Through Effective Leadership.* Englewood Cliffs, NJ: Prentice Hall.

Johnson, J. (1993). *Turning the Thing Around.* New York: Hyperion.

Loder, J.I. (1981). *The Transforming Moment: Understanding Convictional Experiences.* San Francisco: Harper & Row.

Mezirow, J. (Ed.). (1990). *Fostering Critically Reflection in Adulthood.* San Francisco: Jossey-Bass.

Mezirow, J. (1991). *Transformative Dimensions of Adult Learning.* San Francisco: Jossey-Bass.

Satir, V. (1972). *The New Peoplemaking.* Palo Alto, CA: Science and Behavior Books.

Satir, V., Stachowiak, J; Taschman, H.A. (1975). *Helping Families to Change.* New York: James Arnson.

Schlossberg, N.K. (1984). *Counseling Adults in Transition.* New York: Springer.

Sherman, E. (1987). *Meaning in Mid-Life Transition.* Albany NY: State University of New York Press.

CHAPTER 3

Allen, J. (1990). *I Saw What You Did & I Know Who You Are.* Tucker, GA: Performance Management.

CHAPTER 4

Crosby, P. (1992). *Completeness: Quality for the 21st Century.* New York: Dutton.

Crosby, P. (1990). *Quality is Free.* New York: Penguin.

Deming, W. Edwards. (1993). *The New Economics.* Cambridge, MA: Massachusetts Institute of Technology Center for Advanced Engineering Study.

Deming, W. Edwards. (1986). *Out of the Crisis.* Cambridge, MA: Massachusetts Institute of Technology Center for Advanced Engineering Study.

Dobyns, Lloyd, and Crawford-Mason, Clare. (1991). *Quality or Else.* Boston, MA: Houghton Mifflin.

Feigenbaum, A. (1988). *The Rise of the Expert Company.* New York: Times Books/Random House.

Feigenbaum, A. (1990). *Total Quality Control.* New York: McGraw-Hill.

Gabor, Andrea. (1990). *The Man Who Discovered Quality.* New York: Times Books, Random House.

Harrington, H. James. (1987). *The Improvement Process.* New York: McGraw-Hill.

Juran, J.M. (1989). *Juran on Leadership for Quality.* New York: The Free Press.

Juran, J.M. (1988). *Juran on Planning for Quality.* New York: The Free Press.

Juran, J.M. (1988). *Juran's Quality Control Handbook.* New York: McGraw-Hill.

Kilian, Cecelia S. (1988). *The World of W. Edwards Deming.* Washington, DC: CEEPress Books.

Kohn, Alfie, (1993). *Punished by Rewards.* Boston: Houghton Mifflin.

Mann, Nancy R. (1989). *The Keys to Excellence: The Story of the Deming Philosophy.* Los Angeles: Prestwick.

Naisbitt, J. (1990). *Megatrends 2000.* New York: Morrow.

Ouchi, W. (1981). Theory Z: How American Business Can Meet the Japanese Challenge. New York: Addison-Wesley.

Peters, T.; Waterman, R., Jr. (1982). *In Search of Excellence.* New York: Warner.

Peters, T.; Austin, W. (1985). *A Passion for Excellence.* New York: Random House.

Peters, Tom, (1991). "Tom Peters Live." Boulder, CO: Career Track Publication.

Scherkenbach, William W. (1990). *The Deming Route to Quality and Productivity.* Rockville MD: Mercury Press.

Walton, Mary. (1986). *The Deming Management Method.* New York: Putnam.

CHAPTER 5

Bandler, R. and Grinder, J. (1979). *Frogs into Princes: Neuro-Linguistic Programming.* Moab UT: Real People Press.

Bandler, R. and Grinder, J. (1976). *The Structure of Magic I and II.* Palo Alto: Science and Behavior Books.

Briggs-Myers, I. (1980). *Gifts Differing.* Palo Alto, CA: Consulting Psychologist Press.

Dilts, R., et al. (1980). *Neuro-Linguistic Programming.* Cupertino CA: Meta Publications.

Dyer, Wayne W. (1989). *You'll See it When You Believe it.* New York: Morrow.

Elgin, Suzette Haden. (1993). *Genderspeak: Men, Women and the Gentle Art of Verbal Self-Defense.* New York: John Wiley.

Glass, Lillian. (1992). *He Says She Says: Closing the Communication Gap Between the Sexes.* New York: Putnam.

Gray, J. (1992). *Men Are from Mars, Women Are from Venus.* New York: Harper Collins.

Hirsh, S. (1985). *Using the Myers-Briggs Type Indicator in Organizations.* Palo Alto, CA: Consulting Psychologist Press.

Hirsh, S. and Kummerow, J. (1989). *Lifetypes.* New York: Warner Books.

Kiersey, D. & Bates, M. (1984). *Please Understand me: An Essay on Temperament Styles.* Del Mar, CA: Prometheus Nemesis Press.

Kroeger, O. with Thusen, J. (1992). *Type Talk at Work.* New York: Delacorte Press.

McClelland, D.C. (1985). *Human motivation.* Glenview, IL: Scott Foresman.

Moir, A. and Jessel, D. (1991). *Brain Sex: The Real Difference Between Men and Women.* Secaucus, NJ: Carol Group.

Palmer, H. (1988). *The Enneagram: Understanding Yourself and Others.* New York: Harper & Row.

Robbins, A. (1991). *Awaken the Giant Within.* New York: Summit.

Robbins, A. (1986). *Unlimited Power.* New York: Simon and Schuster.

Tannen, D. (1990). *You Just Don't Understand.* New York: Ballantine.

CHAPTER 6

Blanchard, K. (1990). *The One Minute Manager Builds High Performing Teams.* New York: Morrow.

Hale, R.L. and Maehling, R.F. (1992). *Recognition Redefined.* Minneapolis: Tennant Company.

LeBoeuf, M. (1985). *The Greatest Management Principle in the World.* New York: Putnam.

Peters, Tom. (1992). *Liberation Management.* New York: Knopf.

Petersen, D. (1991). *A Better Idea: Redefining the Ways Americans Work.* Boston: Houghton Mifflin.

Quick, T. (1992). *Successful Team Building.* New York: AMACOM.

Riley, P. (1993). *The Winter Within: A Life Plan for Team Players.* New York: Putnam.

Sher, B. and Gottlieb, A. (1989). *Teamworks.* New York: Warner Books.

CHAPTER 7

Ash, M.K. (1984). *Mary Kay on People Management.* New York: Warner Books.

Beattie. Melody. (1989). *Beyond Codependency and Getting Better.* New York: Harper & Row.

Bernstein, Paula (1985). *Family Ties/Corporate Bonds.* New York: Doubleday.

Goddard, R.W. (1984). "Motivating the Modern Employee." *Management World* 13, no. 2.

Graham, G. (1990). "The Motivational Impact of Nonfinancial Employee Appreciation Practices on Medical Technologies." *Health Care Supervisor* 8(3).

Kovach, K. (1980). "Why Motivational Theories Don't Work." *Advanced Management Journal* 45, no. 2.

McCormick, E.J., and Ilgen, D.R. (1980). *Industrial Psychology.* Englewood Cliffs, NJ: Prentice Hall.

Mellody, Pia. (1989). *Facing Codependence.* San Francisco: Perennial Library.

Nelson, Bob, (1984). *1001 Ways to Reward Employees.* New York: Worman.

Nichols, Ted, (1993). *Secrets of Entrepreneurial Leadership.* Dearborn, MI: Enterprise.

Pietropinto, Anthony. (1986). "The Workaholic Spouse." *Medical Aspects of Human Sexuality.* V20(5). pp. 89–96.

Schaef, Anne Wilson (1985). *Codependence: Misunderstood, Mistreated.* Minneapolis: Winston.

Schaef, Anne Wilson (1987). *When Society Becomes an Addict.* San Francisco: Harper Row.

Schaef, Anne Wilson, and Fassel, Diane (1988). *The Addictive Organization.* New York: Harper Collins.

Wegscheider-Cruse, Sharon. (1984). *"Codependency: The Therapeutic Void." Health Communications.* pp. 1–4.

Zemke, Ron. (1989). "Reward and Recognition: Yes, They Really Work."*Training.* pp. 49–53.

Zemke, Ron. (1990). *The Service Edge.* New York: Penguin.

INDEX